FIRE

IN THE WAX MUSEUM

Melting Our Hearts With the Flame of His Presence

FIRE

IN THE WAX MUSEUM

Melting Our Hearts With the Flame of His Presence

REV. BUD WILLIAMS

Treasure House

An Imprint of
Destiny Image® Publishers, Inc.
P.O. Box 310
Shippensburg, PA 17257-0310

"For where your treasure is,
there will your heart be also." Matthew 6:21

ISBN 1-56043-344-2

For Worldwide Distribution
Printed in the U.S.A.

This book and all other Destiny Image, Revival Press,
and Treasure House books are available
at Christian bookstores and distributors worldwide.

For a U.S. bookstore nearest you, call 1-800-722-6774.
For more information on foreign distributors, call 717-532-3040.
Or reach us on the Internet: http://www.reapernet.com

Dedication

For the most special character in my life...my wife, Fran.

Acknowledgments

No one, except maybe God, is more appreciative than I of all the encouragement and support it has taken to produce *Fire in the Wax Museum*. I would like to thank the Lord and all His helpers for making it happen.

First, I want to thank my bishop, The Rt. Rev. John W. Howe, for his prayers and his support of my evangelistic ministry. Bill and Carolyn De Arteaga helped distill the raw material and kept me motivated. If it had not been for Rodney Howard-Browne's faithful response to the call of God, the torch of revival would not have been brought from South Africa to the United States, and eventually to Lakeland...thanks, Rodney and Adonica. The parishioners of Christ the King who welcomed the move of God were especially brave and discerning, putting up with radical changes and my imperfections.

My wife's degree from Florida State University in social work proved invaluable, although she has had only one case in her long career—me. I would never have survived 18 years in the pastoral ministry, much less the challenge of organizing and composing a book, without her. Thanks, Fran, for being the best helpmate God could have created for me and the best mom for Elizabeth and Hugh.

Finally, I am indebted to those who contribute to the support our ministry. Your financial support bought time to write, and your prayers paved the way.

Contents

Preface

*But mark this: There will be terrible times in the last days. Peo-
ple will be lovers of themselves, lovers of money, boastful, proud,
abusive, disobedient to their parents, ungrateful, unholy, without love, unforgiving, slanderous, without self-control, brutal,
not lovers of the good, treacherous, rash, conceited, lovers of
pleasure rather than lovers of God—having a form of godliness
but denying its power* (2 Timothy 3:1-5a).

Have you ever been to a wax museum? Usually museums are
stately and impressive; quiet, peaceful, and orderly. The colorful
figures on display are representations of actual people, seemingly
so alive that if you stand and gaze at them for very long, you will
begin to imagine that they are moving slightly. Yet, one touch will
reveal that they are cold and frozen; one scratch below the surface
will show that their lifelike appearance is but an illusion. The wax
figures have the *look* of life and the *form* of vitality, but the power
of true life is absent.

Many churches are like wax museums. Their orderliness, familiar traditions, and comfortable routines create the appearance

of life and vitality. A closer look, however, reveals that these churches, like the wax figures in the museum, have become cold and frozen in their traditions and routines, unmoved by the Spirit of God and insensitive to His voice. They have "a form of godliness" but lack true spiritual power or any real sense of the Lord's presence. What happens when God kindles a *fire in the wax museum*?

Christians know God as present, personal, and powerful. What happens when He steps closer and becomes *more present, more personal*, and *more powerful* than we ever imagined? What happens when He comes as a refining fire, melting away the wax of tradition? What happens when God brings *revival*?

Some pray for a revival like the Great Awakening, the Welsh Revival, or Azusa Street. Others prophesy that revival is on the way. Still others schedule so-called "revival meetings" each spring and fall. Our congregation did none of that, but in March of 1993, the Wind of Heaven swept down upon us, shaking the whole church with the presence and power of Jesus in a way we had never known. God's holy fire swept through the wax museum of our comfortably charismatic church and changed us forever. It left many of us wondering, like St. Mary, just "what kind of greeting this might be."[1]

Fire in the Wax Museum chronicles the Lakeland Revival and its effect on a contented, traditional American congregation, and its spread to other churches around the world. Oddly enough, it was *contentment* that God seemed most determined to purge from us. He extended the invitation to push our boat into deeper water, and when the church accepted it, everything changed—our families, our church, and our ministry. Remarkably and simultaneously, the same changes happened to other pastors and churches all over the world.

1.　"Mary was greatly troubled at his words and wondered what kind of greeting this might be" (Lk. 1:29).

When my wife, Fran, looks back to the beginning of the revival, she says, "God dropped a bomb on our church." The element of surprise was strategic, because if we had known in advance what an upheaval the move of God would cause in our congregation, we might never have surrendered control. Having tasted the fruit of revival, however, we know we can never return to church as usual—nor do we wish to.

Revival transmits fresh anointing that is wonderfully transferable and available upon request, unlimited by denomination, country, or continent. Those who seek, find.

Repentance and *change* are synonyms for *revival.* Jesus changes His Church. The Good Shepherd shears away the woolly traditions of men, a ticklish shearing that makes some of the sheep skittish. Sheep who submit to the process, however, find themselves free to run and play once the burdensome fleece is removed and wool no longer covers their eyes.

When revival is received and given time to mature, it brings permanent changes, first to people, then to churches, and eventually to society for generations to come. Where revival is rejected (and it often is), things remain as they were or continue their slow state of deterioration.

Revival is not simply an emotional balm for enthusiastic believers, any more than religion is, as Karl Marx declared, the opium of the people. At its core, revival is a refreshed relationship with Jesus. Like any relationship, it cannot be fully appreciated by analysis; it must be experienced as a personal encounter.

Today, thousands of congregations worldwide are experiencing revival. A fresh anointing of the Holy Spirit is falling from Heaven, transferred through the laying on of hands, and sometimes sovereignly, from the hand of God Himself. Millions have received a fresh touch from the Lord when, after simply hearing about revival, they said, "Yes! That's what I want." Countless lives have been changed in the twinkling of an eye after hearing an audio tape, viewing a video, or reading about the current move of God.

I pray that God will touch your life as you read this book, and that you will grow in your hunger and thirst for a closer relationship with God through Jesus Christ our Lord in the power of the Holy Spirit. I pray that God's firey presence melts the frozen traditions of men and kindles fresh fire in the heart of His people.

Foreword

Fire in the Wax Museum is the story of an Episcopal priest, a minister of a parish in the central Florida town of Lakeland, and his journey into revival—into a personal revival as well as a ministry of leading others into revival.

Father Bud Williams was comfortable in his position as pastor when suddenly he was arrested by the Holy Spirit and catapulted right out of his comfort zone. Bud left the church as the pastor and stepped out to begin to "walk on the water," embarking on a Holy Spirit adventure that has taken him around the world.

Until the Lord touched him, who would have believed that he and I would be associated both as friends and as ministers of this unusual ministry! I count it a joy to know Father Bud; his sense of humor is uplifting and his outlook on life refreshing.

Father Bud and his family are members of our church—The River at Tampa Bay—and I am excited at what the Lord is doing in and through their lives. I believe that what you are about to read is only the beginning of what God is going to do in and through them.

Enjoy this book as you get a revelation of how the Holy Spirit can bring a fire into your wax museum!

Dr. Rodney M. Howard-Browne
Tampa, Florida

Chapter One

The Day the Fire Fell

We have seen His glory...(John 1:14b).

"Glory to You, Lord Christ," the congregation replied out of habit when the Gospel reading was announced. Customarily, liturgical churches like ours omit the congregational responses during the Palm Sunday service, but this particular Palm Sunday marked a departure from tradition in many ways. Suddenly, as the people spoke the word *glory*, the glory of the Lord fell upon the whole congregation at once.

The same "rushing mighty wind" that had swept me off my feet in a personal revival at a neighboring church descended in power upon my congregation. Although we were a charismatic church and thus acquainted with the ways and work of the Holy Spirit, such a dramatic manifestation of His presence in our midst was totally unexpected. We greeted His arrival with mixed emotions, much as we would an uninvited guest. His coming forced us to make abrupt choices and radical changes.

For liturgical churches such as the Episcopal Church, Palm Sunday marks the beginning of Holy Week. It is a "red-letter day" on the historical church calendar, with red symbolizing the blood of Christ. According to custom, we had decorated the church with palm trees and that morning joyfully processed into the sanctuary waving palm branches just as the crowd who greeted Jesus upon His entry into Jerusalem had done. As usual, some women had fashioned lapel crosses out of palm fronds and pinned them on the parishioners as they arrived for worship. It was a festive atmosphere with all the expected symbols in place.

Traditionally, church attendance is higher on Palm Sunday than on most other Sundays, and this spring day in 1993 was no exception. The ushers greeted a throng of visitors as well as a handful of "C & Es," that is, Christmas and Easter Christians. Some "C & Es" also show up on Palm Sunday so that no one in the congregation will greet them on Easter Day with a big Gomer Pyle-like drawl, "Go-o-o-lly, look what the cat drug in." Visitors, "C & Es," regular members—*the more the merrier*, I thought. Christ the King Episcopal Church was ready. The stage was set for a very merry Palm Sunday, indeed.

A Cloud of Glory

Our service began in the usual way with 20 minutes of praise choruses, after which we turned our attention to the reading of the Word. The deacon who usually read the Gospel was absent, so I read the lesson from the lectern. That is when God took over. As one member of the congregation recalls:

> "Father Bud stood at the lectern, raised the Bible, and pronounced, 'The Gospel of the Lord.' What usually followed was a rote response, but that day the church responded with vigor, 'Glory to You, Lord Christ!' True to His Word, the glory came! A quiet peace settled over us. A warmth as thick as honey covered my husband and me. Although I am sure I was breathing, I was unaware of

it. Father Bud slowly melted from the pulpit until he lay face down on the floor. How long we continued in that holy silence, I don't remember. I do know that on that Sunday morning, Jesus came and touched me. It was on that Sunday that I began to change."

As pastor, strangely enough, it would be several months before I discovered that the glory of the Lord had covered the entire congregation that morning. At the time, I was aware only of what was happening to me. As the glory descended upon me, I stopped speaking, physically unable to continue reading. Cerebral faculties churned away in the background as I tried frantically to account for the failure of my vocal cords, but it was of no use. My sensory and cognitive abilities had not ceased to function, however; if anything, they were working overtime trying to comprehend exactly what was happening. The glory of God simply eclipsed them both.

The only thing I could see was the Bible lying on the lectern in front of me. The words were legible, but a veil of light like a mist obscured everything else. Time seemed to stand still as a heavy, invisible weight pressed down on my head. It was as though I had stepped over to "the other side"—had crossed from earth to Heaven. My soul stood frozen in time and space while my spirit whirled like a tornado, soaring ever higher and higher above the earth.

A heavenly hush fell over the congregation—a reverent sense of awe. I was supposed to be reading the Gospel lesson as I had done for decades, yet now it felt unfamiliar to me. It was almost like a childhood memory, as though years had passed since I had last done it. Even more odd was the fact that reading the lesson suddenly seemed unimportant. God's glory in the house—the splendor and majesty of His tangible presence—took priority. Holy silence was more appropriate than holy words. The overwhelming sensation of God's presence claimed center stage, pushing everything else to the side.

My frantic, frustrated mind screamed out for answers to its questions: *Shouldn't I try to read the lesson? Could I even read it if I tried?* However, the presence of the glory seemed to make even the questions irrelevant. Standing still and doing nothing seemed best. There was no apparition of angels or vision of Jesus. I did not consciously think about God. Instead, I was caught up in a trance, like Peter in the Book of Acts.[1]

In her book *Glory, A Jerusalem Experience*, Ruth Heflin described the appropriate response to the presence of God's glory:

"Praise until the spirit of worship comes; worship until the glory comes, then stand in the glory."[2]

Laughing at the Lectern

Within moments, even standing became a problem. My feet slipped backward as though pulled from behind. Instinctively, I tightened my grip on the lectern to keep from falling. Occasionally in the past, I had fallen under the Spirit's power when charismatic ministers prayed for me, but falling while performing my normal priestly duties was unthinkable. I began to fight and argue with God. *You can't do this to me—not now, not here! I'm supposed to be reading the Gospel for Heaven's sake! Lord, surely You can't mean to interrupt the reading of Your own words!* Finally, out of sheer frustration, **Lord, You wrote this stuff!**

My desperate protests went without reply. Slowly I sank to the floor, arguing with God every inch of the way and worrying about what people were thinking. My fingers clutched the lectern like a rock climber gripping the edge of a cliff. I was afraid to let go, afraid to yield to the Spirit in front of my congregation. The "pastor" part of me feared they might think I was having a heart attack.

---

1. "He became hungry and wanted something to eat, and while the meal was being prepared, he fell into a trance" (Acts 10:10).
2. Ruth Ward Heflin, *Glory, A Jerusalem Experience* (Hagerstown, Maryland: The McDougal Publishing Company, 1990), xii.

4

The "evangelist" in me was alarmed at the thought of upsetting visitors, while my "teacher" mentality was sure that some people would not understand (a safe bet considering *I* did not understand *either*). The "prophet" in me discerned that God was doing something new, but I fought it nonetheless. My only comfort was the vague recollection of what had happened when Solomon brought the ark of the covenant into the newly finished temple of the Lord.

> *...then the house was filled with a cloud, even the house of the Lord; so that the priests could not stand to minister by reason of the cloud: for the glory of the Lord had filled the house of God* (2 Chronicles 5:13-14 KJV).

Of course, I knew the Scripture that says, "Jesus Christ is the same yesterday and today and forever,"[3] but I had no idea that God still did things like that. It is a humorous story now, but it was not funny then. At the time, my experience caused me to question both my job security and my sanity. I could just imagine an usher dialing 911: "Please hurry, and bring one of those white jackets with the extra long sleeves!" Off I would go to the mental ward, with no lack of congregation members ready to sign their names to have me committed. I could hear them now: "Father Bud just flipped out! He lost it totally—a complete nervous breakdown right in the middle of church!"

As the anointing grew stronger and the invisible weight continued to press down on my head, I had to make a choice: either let go of the lectern or pull it over on top of me. I chose the former. Releasing my grip, I collapsed to the floor. There I was, a fully vested priest lying spread-eagle on the chancel floor, white robes twisted one way, a bright red clerical stole tossed to the other side. It was a most undignified posture. I thought of the words of John the Baptist: "He must increase, but I must decrease."[4]

---

3.   Heb. 13:8.
4.   Jn. 3:30 (KJV).

Despite my public embarrassment, I started laughing—not a quiet chuckle, which might have been a graceful way to recover from the fall, but sidesplitting belly laughter. Screaming and hooting, I turned my face to the gray tile floor. The joy of the Lord was blatantly manifested, but I could not imagine why God would do such a thing, especially at one of the most solemn moments of the liturgy.

A peculiar laughter roared from deep inside my spirit. Was this what Jesus meant when He promised, "Blessed are you who weep now, for you will laugh"?[5] Although it was yet too soon to tell, the laughter was a turning point. The fat was in the fire. The cat was out of the bag. Revival had come and we would never be the same.

Everyone Was Hit

Surrounded as I was by the cloud of glory, I was unaware of the manifestations occurring throughout the sanctuary. That morning, my wife, Fran, was playing guitar and singing on the worship team. When the glory fell, she began to laugh so hard that it embarrassed her. Bursting out with guffaws in the middle of church was unbefitting a "cradle Episcopalian," so she tried to hide among the palm trees that decorated the front of the church. Others were laughing as well, but I did not hear any of it. The Holy Spirit was moving throughout the congregation. One member, a salesman who was one of our chalice bearers that morning, remembers what happened and some of the aftereffects.

> "It is rather difficult to try to explain just what God did that Sunday. The service started out as usual, but then the Holy Spirit came into our presence and began to respond to all the people who were looking for a fresh touch from the Lord. The service became supercharged as the Spirit worked. It was as if the church had become electrified,

---

5.   Lk. 6:21b.

empowered, set on fire. Time no longer had any meaning. The 'thing' that had taken over was the total worship of God! People were healed physically, emotionally, and spiritually. Some were given gifts of the Spirit. As with any move of God, there were some who just didn't understand what had taken place.

"I do know that as a result of God's anointing, Christ the King Episcopal Church was never quite the same. It was as if no one cared how long the worship service lasted. God be praised. All the services that followed were on fire for the Lord. The worship of God became deeper, and we became more trusting and more accepting of the will of God for our lives. We wanted to share with others what God was doing for us because we knew that He could do the same for them."

Meanwhile, I still struggled on the floor. On a normal Sunday in a liturgical church, there are any number of people ready and available to assist the priest: lay readers, chalice bearers, acolytes. If I dropped a communion wafer or spilled wine, or if a candle went out, someone always came running. However, on Palm Sunday, 1993, the day the fire fell and the Spirit pushed me to the floor, no help was in sight because the glory of the Lord had immobilized the helpers as well. Finally, I was able to catch the eye of one of the readers and signaled for assistance. He helped me to my feet and held me upright while I read the lengthy Passion Gospel.

The whole incident was over within a few minutes. Later, as we reflected on the meaning of that Sunday, we realized that God's passion for His people has not changed. He let us know in a dramatic way that He still wants to glorify Himself among us. We also had a lot of questions: *What next? Was this a once-in-a-lifetime occurrence? Why did this happen? What was the purpose behind it?*

A Second Helping

The following Sunday, Easter Day, people were still talking about what had happened the week before. They spoke as if it were an historical event. No one expected a repeat performance, especially on the holiest day of the Christian calendar.

As usual, visitors and "C & Es" supplemented our regular members to fill the sanctuary for the Easter service. In preparation for this holiest of days, the altar guild had replaced the previous week's palm trees with dozens of Easter lilies, which drenched the sanctuary with their strong, sweet perfume.

"Alleluia. Christ is risen!" The foolproof, beautiful, traditional Easter liturgy began right on schedule.

With broad smiles, the congregation responded with spirit. "The Lord is risen indeed! Alleluia!"

It was time for the Gospel reading. Once again, the deacon was absent; so, amid chuckles from those who had witnessed the events of the previous Sunday, I approached the lectern to read in his place. I smiled too, thinking, *Okay, fair enough. After all, the captain did fall off the bridge last Sunday. That deserves a laugh or two, but there is no way it is going to happen again!* At that point, I should have remembered the old time-tested proverb, "Never say 'never' to God," but I didn't.

As I began to read from the Gospel of John, the same giant, invisible weight pressed down on me just as it had the week before. My head began to tingle and I was struck dumb. This time, I could hear laughter breaking out all over the congregation as the glory cloud descended like a thick fog. Two lay readers rushed to stand behind me.

Thanks fellas, I thought, *but that won't be....* I fell swiftly backward into their arms, and they lowered me to the floor. This time, however, I could not get up. I was stuck to the cold tile floor with Holy Ghost "Superglue." I signaled one of the readers to take my

8

place at the lectern. He tried hard to read the Gospel lesson but had a tough time speaking over the exuberant, joyful laughter. The whole congregation was involved: visitors, old-timers, and new-comers alike.

At first, all I could think about was that I had ruined Easter for dozens of families. On second thought, however, my prophetic instinct wondered how many people had actually come to celebrate the resurrection of Jesus. How many thought He was still on the cross or in the tomb? How many came because of family pressure? Who among them thought they were doing God a favor, discharging a religious duty, or complying with Episcopal doctrine? Previously, I had dismissed such questions from my mind and pretended to be happy to see every soul, even the "C & Es." Now, however, we were within the veil of the glory of God, and ritual could not camouflage the reality of the resurrection. Jesus Christ was undeniably present; He was smack dab in the middle of our Easter service doing exactly the kind of thing that caused His arrest and crucifixion the first time. *He was rocking our theological boat!*

Gasp! Were we actually going to experience what it was like to be a disciple? We had long prayed to be a New Testament church, but the extreme consequences of being a disciple were just beginning to dawn on us. The Spirit's disruption of our well-ordered service embarrassed us, just as Jesus' disciples must have been embarrassed when He spit on someone's eyes to heal them or drove a legion of demons into a herd of pigs. Little did we know that in the weeks ahead, the power of the Lord would continue to manifest. We would see signs, wonders, and miracles—not only in our own congregation, but far beyond parish walls.

A few weeks earlier we had been spectators looking longingly up toward Heaven. Now, Heaven had come down into our midst. Before, our church had been like a wax museum, where familiar figures represented for us the traditional, the comfortable, and the charismatic religion. Now, the fire of God had fallen and had melted us, remolded us, and changed us forever.

9

Chapter Two

Slain in the Coliseum

The revival that fell on Christ the King Episcopal Church on Palm Sunday, 1993 was only a small part of a much greater movement of God that hit central Florida that spring and eventually became labeled the "Lakeland Revival." Carpenter's Home Church was ground zero for the Holy Ghost bombshell that exploded over the area, radiating spiritual shock waves in every direction like ever-widening ripples on a calm lake. Dozens of comfortable, musty "wax museums" were set on fire, and thousands of people were profoundly touched by God. Six years later, the effects are still being felt by people all around the world.

For me, it all began one cool spring Sunday morning when a woman in our congregation encouraged all of us to visit Carpenter's Home Church that night to hear a visiting missionary evangelist from South Africa named Rodney Howard-Browne. I had never heard of him. My initial reaction was *Rodney who-who?...from where-where? South Africa? Are the Africans now sending missionaries to America? That'll be the day!*

Carpenter's Home Church was the Pentecostal version of Carnegie Hall. Contemporary Christian musicians and televangelists all played Lakeland's mega-church. *If I'm going to go to Carpenter's,* I thought, *I'll wait for Phil Driscoll, Sandi Patti, or some other "brand-name" ministry. Why go to hear someone I've never heard of?* As far as I was concerned, Rodney Howard-Browne was an unknown, and I was uninterested.

During the evening of that same Sunday, we received a call from our church pianist, who was playing keyboard at Carpenter's Home. He phoned us between the praise and worship sets. "Turn on your radio," he said. "You've got to hear this." Carpenter's Home Church broadcast its worship services over its own radio station, and so, since turning on the radio did not require much effort, we tuned in.

Laughter blared from the speaker in bursts that lasted five or six minutes, interrupted occasionally by a voice with an unfamiliar accent. "It's real, isn't it? It's the Holy Ghost—the 'new wine!' Have a drink!" Lasting much longer than normal church laughter—the kind that follows a joke told from the pulpit—this laughter on the radio also had an unusual lilt to it.

Novel? Yes. Unfamiliar? Not completely. I had heard the so-called "holy laughter" once before at a John Wimber meeting. Uncontrollable laughter had also broken out once in our home-fellowship group, although at the time, we did not recognize it as a spiritual phenomenon.

Admittedly, the strange laughter on the radio made me curious, but not enough so for me to attend the meetings. Besides, I had planned to go on retreat. I was far too busy with my regular routine to notice that a worldwide revival was unfolding in my backyard.

Cracking the Shell

My wife, Fran, however, began attending the weekday meetings, which were called "revival" meetings. Before long, it was clear that she was being blessed. This made me a little jealous, so I changed my mind and went to a morning meeting. I took with me a completely false set of expectations. First, my theological education had honed my mind to dissect the "new teaching." Teaching was the backbone of the charismatic renewal, and I expected to hear the Word of God expounded in revelatory fashion. Therefore, I sat down with pen and notepad in hand, ready to take notes. As it turned out, there were plenty of scriptural quotations, but it was not primarily a teaching meeting. Revival was different.

Second, I expected to hear good preaching. While Pentecostal doctrine sometimes baffled me, there was no denying that Pentecostals excelled in the art of preaching. Rodney Howard-Browne, however, did not preach in the usual sense of the term. He ambled onto the platform 45 minutes after the meeting began, and strolled back and forth while telling stories. His monologue included personal anecdotes, testimony, and an occasional discourse in tongues followed by the interpretation in English. This "revival" was not primarily a preaching meeting.

Third, I expected a hard sell for money at the offering time. It seemed to me that Pentecostals always preached prosperity yet acted as if their next meal depended totally on the love offering. The evangelist did indeed speak at length on stewardship—more than 30 minutes—but he did not pressure anyone. He simply taught on the importance of giving from a biblical and theologically sound perspective. His message was full of fresh illustrations and set the mood for the people to give cheerfully. It was a refreshing change.

Despite the overall lack of emphasis on teaching and preaching, I enjoyed the meeting. A skeptical observer at first, I heard nothing that turned me off. However, I also heard nothing in particular that turned me on either. Although the service continued into mid-afternoon, I left at lunchtime. Two hours was enough for me, so I beat a quiet, hasty retreat while trying to look as though I had to attend to more urgent matters.

The next day I went back to the revival, although I am not sure why. Perhaps I enjoyed sitting in a church without having to worry about whether it was too warm or too cool for someone or if the music was too loud or too soft—the kinds of things that distract pastors in their home churches. For me, the revival was a kind of retreat, not so much a withdrawal from the world as an opportunity to take refuge in the presence of God. I enjoyed the freedom to worship without having to lead. Even more, something was happening inside me that I could not see and would not discover for a week or more. Unnoticed, the hand of God touched me and changed me.

The second morning meeting was a carbon copy of the first. Brother Rodney did not mind arriving 30 or 40 minutes after the meeting began. The service had the same loose format: stories, testimony, and a lengthy teaching on stewardship. Again, I left before the end of the service.

Although I enjoyed both meetings, I assumed that nothing had happened to me. The Spirit seemed to fall in patches of the congregation, provoking laughter in different groups of people, some on my right and some on my left, but I did not experience anything. I also tried to remember where the Bible said anything about laughing. Sure, Sarah laughed, but all the laughers at the meeting were not *pregnant*! I did not fully understand what was happening. Neither did I realize that I was affected simply by being present.

Sometime during those first two revival meetings—I don't know precisely when—the Lord cracked the shell of my self-satisfaction. Brother Rodney asked a question that kept repeating itself in my mind: "Are you hungry for God?" What kind of a question was that? For some months I had been restless, even wondering if it was time to move to another parish. Was my restlessness a sign of hunger for God? I discovered later that it was, but not before God really caught my attention.

14

Hidden in the Briar Patch

The most unusual evening of my life occurred on the Sunday that the Lakeland Revival began its third week. I had been in my office at the church for several hours catching up on some computer work. Since we had no Sunday evening service, I often enjoyed using the time to work without the usual weekday interruptions. Around 7:00 p.m. my wife called, asking if I was coming home for dinner. While I was apologizing for having lost track of the time, there was a knock at the church door.

Andrea was a bright, attractive woman in her 30's who had been a member of our congregation for about a year and had become a close family friend. Always the spontaneous one, she had passed by the church on her way to the revival, seen the light on, and stopped to see if anyone wanted to go with her.

To this day, I do not know why I agreed to return for another revival service. I had already decided that it was not for me and that I was not going back. For some reason, I changed my mind. God must have big, burly angels whose job is to nudge reluctant souls in the direction He wants them to go. I told Fran that instead of coming home right away, I was going to the revival with Andrea. Off I went for my third visit.

When we arrived at Carpenter's Home Church, the service had already begun and all the best seats were taken. The "best seats," in my opinion, were those in the "skeptic zone"–the aisle seats on the back rows. People sitting in the skeptic zone could escape quickly if anything weird started happening, such as snake handling or other strange things. As we entered, I looked around to see if any of the other 6,000 worshipers were distracted and nervous like I was, but it appeared that almost everyone was deeply engaged in the worship and singing vigorously.

Andrea and I found cover in a thicket of people twelve rows from the back, six seats in from the aisle, and three rows above the closest cross aisle. Although not a treasured "skeptic zone" seat, it

15

offered a safe haven in the middle of the crowd, a comfortable spot where I could be an inconspicuous observer. I felt like the fabled "Br'er Rabbit" secure in his briar patch.

Another reason I liked the camouflage was my casual attire— a polo shirt, jeans, and boat shoes—which was a bit too informal for the "Pentecostal Carnegie Hall." Most of the men wore shirts and ties, and many had sport coats. The women were decked out in everything from denim to damask. The principal ladies wore silk, satin, and sequined party dresses and were escorted by men in fashionable suits and the latest style neckties—a veritable "peacock parade." It was a far cry from the old "holiness code" that required Pentecostal women to wear homely dresses that fell below their knees and to keep their hair tied back in buns. Their modern counterparts looked much like anyone else.

Still, mainline Christians, even charismatic ones like me, tend to suffer from two related afflictions: "Pentephobia," the fear of Pentecostals, and "Fundaphobia," the fear of fundamentalists. Quick to tackle theological issues, no matter how thorny, we tend to become close-mouthed and reclusive when confronted with enthusiastic, unashamedly emotional, shouting, foot-stomping sisters and brothers. I was happy to be hidden in the briar patch.

The back of my confirmation certificate lists church rules, one of which states: "You must not talk in church." That sounded like especially good advice at the revival meeting. I wanted to be like Uncle Remus' "Br'er Fox": "He just lay low," and the "Tar-Baby": "She not sayin' nothin'."[1] For some unknown reason, I wanted to be anonymous. Thankful to be out of uniform (no clerical collar) and to have reading glasses as a disguise, I wanted to watch without becoming involved. *Besides*, I thought, *no one could possibly recognize me in this crowd.* No one, that is, except God.

---

1.   Joel Chandler Harris, *Uncle Remus, His Songs and His Sayings* (New York: D. Appleton and Company, 1901), 8.

16

Flushed Into the Open

At first, everything was similar to the previous services I had attended. The praise and worship were great and lasted over an hour. Eventually, "Br'er Rodney" surfaced and began chatting away in his carefree, anecdotal style. He was jovial without telling jokes. Nevertheless, as he spoke, pockets of laughter broke out around the auditorium. Then, suddenly, there was a change in the atmosphere. A spiritual force charged it with electricity, almost as though angel wings were beating the air. An invisible but audible sensation stirred expectancy in the crowd. We sensed that something was about to happen.

For the first time, the evangelist moved away from the platform and into the congregation. Flanked by an entourage of ushers and a video crew, he began to pray for people. "Step into the aisle, dear lady. Fill!" Over she went, falling backward into the arms of the ushers who dashed about like parking valets. Women called "rag ladies" quickly covered the fallen woman with a "modesty cloth"—a three-by-three-foot square of pink fabric placed over exposed ankles and hemlines.

The roving TV camera crew did not miss a shot, and the congregation could see all the action on giant overhead screens. Those near me craned their necks for an eyewitness view, but I felt uncomfortable. *The minister should stay on the platform,* I thought. *If people want prayer, they should choose to go forward. What if someone does not want prayer? Suppose he comes back here to the briar patch where I am hiding?*

Larger waves of laughter rippled through the congregation. Some of it was in reaction to the amusing sight of people toppling, swooning, and dropping to the ground—"slain in the Spirit" as the Pentecostals say—and some of it was a contagious response to the laughter of others. Most of it, however, was a volcano-like eruption of belly laughter. Ecstatic joy exploded in whole sections of the congregation. My "skepticism-meter" was working overtime trying

17

to figure it out, yet somehow—perhaps by discernment—I sensed that it was genuine. Somehow, I knew this was God.

Deeper and deeper into the congregation marched the ministerial convoy. "Step into the aisle. Fill!" "Br'er Rodney" continued. "You, sir, fill. Fill, fill, fill, fill, fill." Rodney marked targets at a faster pace as the spiritual intensity and fervor increased.

Almost everyone in the room was smiling and enjoying themselves. Why did it seem so unusual to see church people rapt in joy? Jesus said, "Blessed are you who weep now, for you will laugh."[2] Still, the experience frustrated me. *Was I supposed to laugh at the absurdity of the situation, or was I to wait for an involuntary reaction? Was it a psychological manifestation, group hysteria, or mass hypnosis? Was there a purpose behind it, or was it merely for fun? Would unbelievers be put off by such extremes, or would they be attracted even more to a God so powerful that He could make people fall down with one invisible blow?* Questions were generated faster than I could answer them.

My thoughts were interrupted by the realization that Howard-Browne and company had reached the back of the auditorium. Although he was still a dozen vertical aisles away, he had ascended to the highest cross aisle—the one that passed just below me. Then the cavalcade turned left and headed in my direction. *Surely he will return to the platform before he comes all the way to the back corner of the auditorium! Please, "Br'er Rodney," don't come back here to the briar patch!*

A battle began between my head and my heart. My intellect wanted to remain aloof and objective. *Go away, Howard-Browne; you've come far enough. Go back to the platform.* My heart, however, made a different plea. *Choose me; pray for me. I want a fresh touch from the Lord. I know I don't deserve it, but I want it!*

---

2.   Lk. 6:21b.

Suddenly, "Br'er Rodney" stood directly in front of the briar patch. Glancing over three rows, his eyes locked with mine in a penetrating stare. He looked over at Andrea, then again at me. I did not know how to respond. Should I acknowledge the stare, feign a smile or a laugh, or look away? I felt paralyzed, like a deer caught in the headlights.

"Br'er Rodney" took a deep breath, pursed his lips, then grinned a "cat-that-swallowed-the-canary" grin. His deep-set tropical blue eyes sparkled with anticipation. "Those four!" he commanded, pointing to Andrea, me, and a woman and a teenage girl behind me. "Bring them out quickly, quickly, quickly. Step into the aisle."

The crowd roared their approval, cheering, clapping, laughing, and nodding their heads. It was as if we were first-century Christians in the Roman Coliseum, cornered by gladiators in the arena. "Emperor Rodney" had ruled "thumbs down," and we were doomed. My head compromised with my heart. I agreed to die—to be "slain in the Spirit"—but to die with dignity, bravely and with no emotion.

Down, But Not Out

The four of us stepped over the others in our rows and into the extra-wide aisle that ran down the north side of the auditorium. As we turned to face the evangelist, we were surrounded instantly by ushers. The camera crew scurried to get set, and the "rag ladies" quietly awaited their cue.

"Lift your hands and receive," demanded the evangelist. As we complied, he bellowed out, "Fill!"

Exactly what happened next, I cannot say. My eyes closed, and suddenly I was lying on my back on the floor, conscious but subdued. My mind frantically analyzed the experience, concluding little more than the fact that I was slain on the floor of the coliseum. I figured that the others were probably dead as well.

Even though I had been "slain in the Spirit" on several occasions before, I still did not fully understand it. For example, why was it called being "slain in the Spirit"? The only people I could think of who were "slain in the Spirit" in the New Testament were Ananias and Sapphira.[3] Augustine, writing in the fourth century A.D., defined the sacraments of Baptism and Communion as "outward and visible signs of an inward and spiritual grace." Although being "slain in the Spirit" was not one of the great sacraments of the Gospel, the experience fit Augustine's description. It was a mystery, a sign, and a wonder. The outward sign was falling into a trance. The inward and spiritual grace, although probably transmitted simultaneously, was not revealed until days later.

So falling was not new to me, but what happened next certainly was. As soon as I hit the floor, I burst into laughter, not just a chuckle or giggle, but robust belly laughter that erupted from deep within me. It was uncontrollable, exploding from my mouth like steam from a train whistle. The laughter was so forceful, in fact, that afterward I was hoarse for two days. God had succeeded in capturing my attention, but for what purpose?

Strangely enough, through all of this I remained fully aware of where I was and what was happening. What I *didn't* know was *why*. Under my back I could feel the scratchy nap of the carpet and the hard floor beneath it. Because I was lying with my head slightly downhill in an aisle that sloped sharply downward from the back of the church to the front, I could feel blood rushing to my head. I could hear the shrieks of laughter coming from my belly *amplified over the P.A. system*! Whenever Brother Rodney found a laugh that particularly intrigued him, he shared it with the congregation by dangling his handheld microphone directly above the lips of his latest victim. How embarrassing! My cover was blown! For days after the meeting, I ran into people who said, "I heard you on the radio Sunday night," or "We saw you on the big screen." It was

---

3.   See Acts 5:1-10.

humorously humiliating. So much for camouflage and the security of the briar patch!

After 20 minutes or so, I stopped laughing, and finally had the nerve to open one eye for a peek. Those who sat on the ends of the pews were doubled over with laughter, enthralled and amused at the four of us on the floor. I was mortified at being part of the entertainment for the evening. Having come only to observe, I now worried about what people would think. Gradually, I regained my "sea legs," righted myself, and crawled back to the pew on my hands and knees. Crawling was a precaution. If I was drunk on what Brother Rodney called "new wine," I did not want to fall again. My pew-mates smiled at my calculated attempt at dignity. Eventually, I was back in the briar patch, camouflaged again.

During all this, my mind was shooting rapid-fire questions. *How long will this laughing last? Why is this happening to me? How long must I lie on the floor? How does this fit in with the doctrine of free will? Am I able to stand up if I want to? Do I even want to? Can I open my eyes? If I open them, will it spoil the miracle? Is this really the Spirit of the Lord coming upon me, or am I caught up in a mass swoon? If this is God, why is He doing it?* I had no answers at the time.

One giant question eclipsed all the others: *What on earth was this all about?* The answer unfolded over the next few months, but one thing was obvious immediately: Something about me had changed. I wondered what it was and what would happen next.

New Priorities

For the next six weeks, I attended every revival meeting, morning and night. The "new wine" did not act like a sedative but, instead, made me more curious. It was not the teaching or the lively new music that hooked me, but the Spirit's anointing. As I was pulled in deeper, my restlessness calmed down and I saw what God was doing. It was like He had opened the floodgates of a great dam, but instead of water, bright beams of glorious light poured

21

forth. God had released a mighty river of revival for His Church, and I simply couldn't get enough of it.

Revival meetings became a part of our household routine, or more precisely, replaced our household routine. Eight to ten hours a day at services forced us to radically reorganize our schedule. Nevertheless, we felt compelled to drop everything and spend our time in the manifest presence of God. Our children, Elizabeth and Hugh, attended some of the meetings, but because of school and their regular bedtime, they usually ordered a pizza and stayed home. Somehow through it all, they managed to have clean clothes and survive the experience just fine.

Attending to our normal household chores became extraordinarily mundane. At one point, the pump on the irrigation system broke, resulting in patches of dead grass all over our yard. After weeds overgrew the flower beds, curious neighbors stopped by to ask what had happened to our beautiful yard and to see if everything was all right. During those weeks, being anywhere but in the revival meetings seemed foolish. We would worry about the yard another time.

The services, especially the morning ones, had a camp meeting atmosphere. Some people brought their entire families. Mothers brought pillows and blankets for the children. Toddlers slept under the pews. Some children colored in coloring books while others played with small toys on the floor. Occasionally, noisy children brought some disapproving glances from adults nearby, but the moms and dads continued to bring backpacks, lunch pails, and bags of toys. The same revival bug that bit me had bitten them. Like Fran and me, they could not stay away.

In the evenings, folks also came prepared to persevere, bringing water bottles, sandwiches, and peppermint candy. Beginning at 7:00 p.m., the services often lasted past midnight. No matter how late they stayed, those who left early always missed something. One night, just before the service, I overheard a woman in front of me dispensing long-distance discipline to her children over her cellular telephone. "No, you may not.... Your brother did what? Put him on the phone.... I'm in church right now, but when I get home...."

More Hunger, More Glory

Most people arrived on time for the lengthy meetings. Getting a seat close to the front, even in the section reserved for pastors, meant arriving when the doors opened an hour before the service. I always tried to arrive early to get as close to the front as possible, and so did scores of others. Worshipers eagerly, almost rudely, rushed in to save seats for their friends. Bibles, purses, and tissues served as seat-occupied cards. Some left after two hours, others after the altar call, but most of the crowds of five to seven thousand per night stayed until the end.

It was difficult to know when the service was over. There was no benediction and only an occasional closing word or "good night." When the evangelist finished praying for everyone and left the platform, the lights were dimmed to encourage everyone to go home. However, many found it impossible to leave. At midnight, the auditorium usually looked like a battlefield. Bodies lay up, down, and across every aisle. The expansive stage and choir area, where Brother Rodney prayed for clergy, was a sea of sobbing, laughing, and rolling ministers, both men and women.

A 30-foot wide foyer was the largest area used for prayer. The corridor encircling the perimeter of the auditorium, one-fifth of a mile in length, was swamped nightly with people in various stages of ecstasy: some stuck to the floor, others to the wall. Hundreds more lay in the enormous atrium-style lobby, and still more around its grand balconies. Bodies covered every square foot of floor space in the vast Carpenter's Home Church.

Hours after the evangelist made his exit, the ministry of the Holy Spirit went on. The heavy anointing continued to immobilize tens of hundreds, and the laughing split the air into the early

23

hours of the morning. Some laughed so loud they could be heard throughout the building. Others, not touched directly by the outpouring of joy, caught the Spirit by osmosis. Every face had a grin or awestruck expression. The dimmed lights created a surreal mood, not frightening or weird, but holy, reverent, and amazing. In the truest sense of the word, it was *glorious.* We all knew that we were in the presence of the Almighty.

Outside the church, another bizarre scene unfolded. People appeared to be drunk. Hundreds staggered to their cars; others could not find their cars. Some required assistance from friends and passersby. It could have been a street scene outside a local barroom at closing time. If the Day of Pentecost looked anything like a revival service, it is little wonder that bystanders thought the disciples were inebriated.

> *Amazed and perplexed, they asked one another, "What does this mean?" Some, however, made fun of them and said, "They have had too much wine." Then Peter stood up with the Eleven, raised his voice and addressed the crowd: "Fellow Jews and all of you who live in Jerusalem, let me explain this to you; listen carefully to what I say. These men are not drunk, as you suppose. It's only nine in the morning! No, this is what was spoken by the prophet Joel: 'In the last days, God says, I will pour out My Spirit on all people...' "* (Acts 2:12-17).

This spiritual intoxication caused me to question my own sanity. *What on earth am I doing in a place like this, not just once, but day after day, night after night, and week after week?* My intellect was too small to grasp the immensity of what was happening. Force of habit made me ask whether it was all of the devil, but spiritual discernment left no doubt in my mind that it was the Spirit of God. Of course, not everything that happens in a revival meeting is of the Spirit of God any more than everything that happens in any church meeting is from God. Nevertheless, I believed it was the best place I could possibly be, basking in the glory of God. In the midst of the chaos, there was peace and joy. The peace passed all understanding, and the joy was unspeakable. I concluded, *This, indeed, is that spoken by the prophet Joel.*

> *And afterward, I will pour out My Spirit on all people. Your sons and daughters will prophesy, your old men will dream dreams, your young men will see visions. Even on My servants, both men and women, I will pour out My Spirit in those days* (Joel 2:28-29).

Another thing I realized, although admitting it was a bit hard on my ego, was that I needed revival. Once, when a member of my congregation tugged on my sleeve during the service to ask what I thought of it all, I remembered what Archbishop Desmond Tutu said to news reporters when apartheid ended in South Africa: "This is not a time to talk. This is a time to dance." I would have plenty to say in my parish on Sunday morning, but at the moment, I needed to worship.

Many questions remained. *How long can this go on? Can you overdo it? How much is enough? Is it only a mountaintop experience? Is it real, or will I awake from a dream? Is the change permanent, or will it fade away?* I was familiar with the ministry of the Holy Spirit through the charismatic renewal, but this was different. God was taking us to a whole new level.

Chapter
Three

A New Church for a New Millennium

Beware lest any man spoil you through philosophy and vain deceit, after the tradition of men, after the rudiments of the world, and not after Christ (Colossians 2:8 KJV).

When word got out that revival had come to an Episcopal church, some people assumed that our congregation had discovered the Holy Spirit for the first time. Actually, ours had been a charismatic parish throughout its eight-year history, and we enjoyed the best of both worlds. We had the balance and stability of a traditional church, the structure of a liturgical church, and the impulsive spontaneity of a Pentecostal church. Our bishop was a Spirit-filled man who understood us, so submitting to his authority was easy. Apart from the Book of Common Prayer, however, we had little in common with non-charismatic Episcopalians.

Some from our denomination looked down their patrician noses and viewed us as "happy clappy," anti-intellectual fundamentalists. Considering the source—frozen, apostate deists[1]—and the fact that Jesus said, "Blessed are you when people insult you, persecute you and falsely say all kinds of evil against you because of Me,"[2] we regarded the criticism as either a compliment or a blessing. We were used to the rebuke and rejection that came from other priests, even in a denomination that prided itself on its tolerance and inclusiveness. Most of our encouragement came not from our own denomination, but from renewal organizations and friendly Pentecostals with whom we huddled under the charismatic umbrella—an umbrella that was starting to fall apart.

The Soil of Revival

By the early years of the 20th century many mainline churches, church scholars, and seminaries had abandoned the familiar warmth of orthodoxy for the cold lifelessness of modernism (liberalism), a heresy that had already been condemned by the Roman Catholic Church. About the same time, God gave birth to the modern Pentecostal movement to counter the errors of modernism. The Welsh and Azusa Street Revivals opened the door for the Holy Spirit to renew the Church, but by and large, the established churches rejected this move of God. What had begun as a general renewal movement for the Church resulted in the formation of new Pentecostal denominations.

American mainline churches began to run out of gas in the 1960's. Since then, most of them have continually declined in membership. The charismatic renewal appeared as fresh fire from Heaven, but again, most church leaders rejected it as an unwelcome

---

1. Deism is belief in the existence of a God on purely rational grounds without reliance on revelation or authority; especially, the 17th- and 18th-century doctrine that God created the world and its natural laws, but takes no further part in its functioning. (*Webster New World Dictionary*, Third College Edition, Simon & Schuster, Inc.,1994).

2. Mt. 5:11.

intrusion, choosing instead to remain safely ensconced in the musty museums of their own tradition.

Unlike the early Pentecostals, many charismatics remained loyal to their denominations, even though the reverse was seldom true. Those who were given the "left foot of fellowship" formed independent charismatic churches, or so-called post-denominational churches. Denominations eventually came to tolerate what they called "werfs"—wild-eyed religious fanatics—but the ennobled church hierarchy did not support the movement and thwarted its growth. "Two things particularly offend church dignitaries. They deplore 'hysterical behavior' in religious meetings. They resent new leadership."[3] Like true revival, the charismatic movement had both. Consequently, old prelates rarely embraced it, and renewal leadership became centered around pastors of "lighthouse churches" or around para-church ministries.

Weekend retreats and conferences helped spread the charismatic message throughout mainline churches. Spirit-filled parishioners returned home with new tongues and other spiritual gifts only to discover an unwritten law—"never on Sunday." For the most part, principal worship services were closed to Pentecostal phenomena, although praise choruses occasionally crept in during communion, even in traditional churches. Most charismatic meetings were "safe sects": quiet, controlled, and cautiously within denominational boundaries. The old guard "museum curators" plowed fire lanes that effectively protected their precious "wax museums" from the flames of change. As early as 1981, renewal leaders like Francis McNutt, an ordained Roman Catholic priest, predicted that the movement was in danger of being "damned by faint praise."

In all fairness, rejection of the charismatics was, in part, their own fault. At their best, they ushered in a restoration of the Holy

---

3. John White, *When the Spirit Comes with Power* (Downers Grove, Illinois: InterVarsity Press, 1988), 39.

Spirit and His gifts. At their worst, they were judgmental, prideful, and prone to spiritual faddism. Instead of being the leaven in the loaf, they were perceived by their more traditional brethren as being half-baked, over-emotional flakes who emphasized tongues and hand raising out of all proportion to the weightier matters of personal holiness and evangelism. Unfortunately, this perception was quite often accurate.

Nevertheless, "God chose the foolish things of the world to shame the wise."[4] Millions came to Christ and into the baptism of the Holy Spirit through the charismatic movement. It affected pastors, priests, and parishioners from every denomination. However, this brush fire of renewal that swept across the dry plains of the Church in the 1960's and 1970's began to abate in the 1980's. One evidence of this was the abundance of "past-tense testimonies": "I was touched by the Holy Spirit 20 years ago...." By the late 1980's, the movement had diminished significantly. Although its leaders attempted to pass the torch to the younger generation, it was too late. Ultimately, the charismatic renewal refreshed the Church at large, but did not revive it. After 30 years, the renewal movement itself was in need of renewal.

Charismatic, But...

Our congregation began in 1984, toward the end of the charismatic heyday. Like many brand-new fellowships, we had people from many different denominational backgrounds, all of whom brought their own traditions and expectations with them. The charismatics and Pentecostals would have been happy to sing all morning long, while the evangelicals waited impatiently for the Bible readings and sermon. The excommunicated Catholics among us tolerated a greater emphasis on worship and the Word while waiting for the real service to begin—Holy Communion. Forbearance was a formidable challenge, but the Spirit brought unity and love for one another.

---

4.   1 Cor. 1:27a.

A New Church for a New Millennium

Typical of many new and small congregations, almost everything was "pastor driven." I felt like a kindergarten teacher, pushing the liturgy along with the loudest voice, "Boys and girls, let us stand and say together the ancient affirmation of our faith in the words of the Nicene Creed, found on page 358 of the Book of Common Prayer—the red book located in the seat pocket of the chair in front of you." The same went for singing. I had to exhort, exhort, exhort. After bulldozing people uphill for two services on Sunday morning, I was totally exhausted, ready for lunch and a long nap.

For eight years my wife, Fran, led the music with her guitar. Normally, we began with 20 or 30 minutes of singing in the three-fast-song, three-slow-song format, displaying the lyrics on the front wall of the sanctuary with an overhead projector. Later, after we acquired a piano player, we began to blend the old with the new by using more music from the hymnal. We prayed for the Spirit to move every Sunday morning, and He did so with prophecy, tongues, interpretations, healing, and singing in the Spirit. I knew of no other charismatic church that was as liberated in worship as we were.

Our style of ministry was not a runaway best-seller in a denomination swaddled in tradition. Nevertheless, during the first eight years, the congregation grew steadily to a membership of 150. Before the revival, Sunday morning attendance averaged about 100, with some people driving an hour to come to church.

We were amused whenever traditional churchmen expecting a typical Anglican liturgy came to visit. "Trads," as we called them, usually arrived overdressed for our casual congregation and were easy to spot, even before their discomfort began to show. Fran and I placed bets, figuratively speaking, on how long they would stay. Apart from the specified places in the liturgy, trads did not speak in church. However, eventually he-trad, covering his mouth with the service bulletin, whispered to she-trad, "Babs, I think we are in the wrong place." Although we were sorry to see anyone leave without giving us a fair chance, we learned to smile wistfully as they tiptoed out during the praise and worship music. Having once been trads ourselves, we understood the old Anglican etiquette maxim, N.O.C.T.—Not Our Cup of Tea.

In those early years, answers to prayer came infrequently. When they did come, we were quick to give God the glory for those answers as well as for the miracles and healings we saw on occasion. Still, we were puzzled as to why we did not see them more often. Was God's power blocked by demonic principalities hovering over the city, as some suggested? Were we too stingy in our giving and outreach to unlock the windows of Heaven's blessing? Was God withholding His favor because we were too apathetic and disobedient? Were we lacking in faith or knowledge? There had to be more, and we hungered and thirsted for it. What was the answer?

Money and Ministry

When I pioneered the church, I assumed that everyone who was born again would tithe. The congregation was taught that the Bible is the Word of God and that one of the principles it reveals is that the tithe belongs to the Lord.[5] Still, only 40 percent of the members tithed. Once, when I expressed my frustration to a neighbor who was also the pastor of a nearby Baptist church, he assured me that I was doing better than average. Nationwide, Bible-believing congregations typically had only 15 to 20 percent tithers. Perhaps it wasn't so bad. Our little congregation, located in a developing area and made up of folks of modest income, had the highest weekly giving per family of any church in our diocese, including some that were located in wealthy areas. Nevertheless, I thought we should do better.

With the help of gifts from outside our parish, we were able to build a building and become self-supporting within five years. That was the expectation for a new congregation in our diocese,

---

5.   See Lev. 27:30; Mt. 23:23.

but few could achieve it. Our goal for giving outside the parish was 20 percent of our budget. From the first day, we sent a tithe to headquarters and tried to give another 10 percent to different local, national, and international ministries.

One fund-raiser for one of the ministries we supported taught us a lesson about giving. During the fund-raising campaign, we observed that the churches who gave the smallest amount outside their parish walls were also the ones with the biggest financial problems. We took this lesson to heart, and God met our needs. We always wanted to do more, but money was always tight.

The year before the Lakeland Revival, our finances worsened. To stay afloat, the vestry eliminated all outside giving and cut salaries. The situation was frustrating, discouraging, and depressing. I was ready to throw in the towel that summer, even to the point of reading the classified ads to look for a new job. Why not close the church, transfer the members to other congregations, sell the property, and give the money to someone who is really flowing in the Spirit? I had visions of my tombstone reading, "He paid the electric bill." If the measure of a church's greatness was in what it gave rather than in what it received, we were a liability to the Kingdom.

Aside from the tithing issue, I also made the false assumption that people who were baptized in the Holy Spirit would eagerly assume their place in some form of service in the life and ministry of the church. Canon law expected the same; part of the minimum requirement for being a member in good standing was working to build up the Kingdom of God. This was easier said than done. Besides a modest per capita income, we had a very small pool of leaders. Those adults who did not work were retirees who took the word *retirement* seriously. Most of them came from traditional church backgrounds that had taught for centuries that the ministers of the church were bishops, priests, and deacons. Although the new catechism added the words *lay persons* to the list of ministers in the church, selling the idea that *every* member was a minister was almost impossible.

This difficulty illuminates one of the problems with charismatics (and non-charismatics as well): They are prone to eating disorders. Week after week, they come to gobble up the Word. If the preacher does not "feed them" to their satisfaction, they leave to graze in greener pastures. Expending their spiritual calories hauling around 25-pound study Bibles and pushing their hands in the air, they are too busy to help with the ministry of the church. Mention the name *Jesus* and they smile and say, "Amen," but rarely do they lead anyone to meet Him or even invite them to church. It is not lack of nourishment; they simply are not motivated.

Locked in the Museum

Almost everyone in our congregation was born again; the majority were baptized in the Holy Spirit and spoke in tongues. Although we considered ourselves evangelical and charismatic, we knew that we did not have the same power as the New Testament Church on the Day of Pentecost. We longed for apostolic experience as well as apostolic teaching; yet ours was a peaceful church with no grumbling, and most people were content. Probably our biggest fault was comparing ourselves to other congregations rather than seeking God's specific will and purpose for *us*.

Selwyn Hughes, the founder of Great Britain's Crusade for World Revival, insists that it is God who sends revival.[6] That was certainly true in our case. Left to ourselves, we would never have asked for the intense and dramatic reforms that genuine revival brings. In our own view, we saw no need to change. Our parish was camped comfortably on the charismatic plain.

Theoretically, we knew that Jesus wanted followers, not merely campers. God is always moving, and each day we are faced with

6. Selwyn Hughes, "Revival-Times of Refreshing" (Middlesex, England: CWR, 1990).

34

the choice to either follow Him or be left behind. Sometimes it seems much easier simply to drop out of the procession, pitch a tent, and stay put; but in so doing, we risk missing the glory of God. Following God is more difficult and requires more discipline and commitment, but the rewards are worth it.

Congregations are made up of people, and unfortunately, people do not change easily. As pastor, I found accepting the sheep as they were much easier than trying to lead them to greener pastures. Starting a new congregation is the most rewarding and exhausting job in the church; and after eight years at the parish, I was both satisfied and exhausted. I saw no need and had no desire to change. At the time, I was unconscious of my burned-out spiritual condition, languid marriage, and degenerated family relationships.

Although I did not see my fatigue, others in the congregation did and began to pray for me privately. Did prayer bring revival, or did the dawn of revival stir the faithful? It is hard to say. Looking back, I do recall an increase in intercession and petition, but no one mentioned revival. Even if we had known what genuine revival was, I doubt that it would have made the prayer list.

If someone had told us at the time that our church was frozen in charismatic tradition, we would have denied it, but it was true nonetheless. As proud of our charismatic tradition as the mainline churches were of their history and convention, subconsciously we had locked the doors and withdrawn to the main gallery of our wax museum, where we hunkered down to wait for Jesus' return.

Moving the Liturgical Mountain

The revival that fell upon us beginning on Palm Sunday, 1993 immediately posed new challenges and raised new questions for us. In time, the Spirit of the Lord answered every one, but I have to admit that I worried until those answers came. The first and biggest question was how to open up and welcome the Holy Spirit while at the same time remain loyal to the traditional worship of the Episcopal Church. How could we integrate revival into a liturgical service? Was it even possible?

The liturgy—the order of service—is the backbone of Anglican churches, and it was no different with us. We celebrated Holy Communion every Sunday according to the tradition passed on to us in the Book of Common Prayer. Although other Christians sometimes teased us about reading "canned prayers," most of our people found comfort and security in the formal, repetitive cadences that the Church has used for centuries. It offered consolation at funerals, cheer at weddings, and weekly encouragement in a denomination not particularly well known for preaching. By definition, the liturgy is the epitome of tradition. It was the first mountain we had to move if we were honestly going to flow with the Holy Spirit.

To many in the church, the idea of changing the service, which is read entirely from a book dating back to 1559, smacked of heresy. Most of the congregation preferred a predictable service and became even more passionate about the liturgy after revival broke out. Once, in an attempt to shorten the 10:00 a.m. service, I suggested cutting out some of the optional prayers and Bible readings, but the congregation would have none of it.

Wisdom said to leave the 8:00 a.m. hour-long Holy Communion service alone. It attracted 20 or so regulars who came for a variety of reasons. After the revival began, this "early bird special," as we called it, also became a nesting place for refugees fleeing the rapidly changing 10:00 a.m. service. Of course, having a church where everyone was in revival would have been ideal, but a little leaven in the loaf was enough to raise the spiritual level of the whole congregation. The early service was also an entrance door for those being drawn to the church. It remained essentially the same, although occasionally, someone would "fall out" when prayed for at the communion rail. In this sense, revival penetrated every area of the church.

A New Church for a New Millennium

The main service at 10:00 a.m. was the real test. If we were serious when we said, "Come, Holy Spirit and have Your way with us," it meant laying everything on the altar: the music, the timetable, and even the liturgy. I gave the congregation fair warning that there was no guarantee they would receive communion at the main service. Considering the circumstances, who could predict what the Spirit would do next? As it turned out, we never missed communion and were completely faithful to the liturgy of the church.

The biggest change came not from what we took away but from what we added. People wanted more praise and worship, altar calls, and the laying on of hands every Sunday. In many ways, it was a pastor's dream; in another, his worst nightmare—it added a lot more time to the service. The main service was already pushing two hours, but with the expanded liturgy, it frequently lasted more than three. I knew this was hard on mothers with young children, elderly folk, and those who could not sit for a long time. One man complained regularly about missing the buffet at the retirement home. It was a problem that only God could solve, and He did so.

A revelation struck like a thunderbolt: The members of the congregation were grownups! If they could not sit, they were free to move around. If the service ran too long for them, they were free to leave or to come to the early bird special. If someone missed his lunch, he could either go to McDonald's® afterwards or bring a sack lunch with him. The point is, we stopped trying to please and manipulate people and sought instead to reverence God and yield to whatever He desired to do in the church.

This revelation was hard for me in a way because it forced me to confront the way I had managed the Sunday service for years. Had I tried to please people instead of God? Did I manipulate people? Was I more concerned with the length of the service than with worshiping the Lord? Yes. I was guilty on all charges. However, there was no condemnation, only a chance to repent and follow

God. What joy and freedom came from not having to produce a performance on Sunday! Now I attended church with a new enthusiasm, simply to see what the Lord was going to do next.

Navigating the River of Change

Liturgical services offer a balanced approached to worship, but weekly manifestations of the Holy Spirit threw us off kilter. For one thing, it became impossible to publish the usual church bulletin because we never knew in advance what to expect. The best we could do was to print a warning in the weekly handout, advising visitors that the church was "under construction" and describing some of the spiritual phenomena that they might encounter, such as outbreaks of joyous laughter and falling to the ground. It also provided a brief explanation of the more familiar manifestations of speaking in tongues, interpretation of tongues, prophecy, words of wisdom and knowledge, and healing.

Some members were afraid that such spiritual manifestations as these might be off-putting to newcomers, when in fact, the opposite was true. More often than not, it was the church people who were offended. Newcomers were looking for something that was missing from their lives—God—and when they found Him alive and well and working in the lives of real people, they were intrigued.

One problem that surfaced early on was how to clear the church after the service was over. This was due to two factors. First, after the glory fell, the power of the Lord continually filled our church. Frequently, it was so strong that some people were stuck to the floor even after the three-hour service, while others were too weak-kneed to walk. To solve this, the ushers put to use a wheelchair that a widower had given to the church some months earlier after his wife died. The "slain" were simply wheeled to their cars. What we had once considered a white elephant proved to be a prophetic gift!

The second difficulty in clearing the church was the fact that folks tended to linger and talk long after the service ended. You would think that after three hours or more, they would be anxious to leave, but they were so excited about what God was doing that all they wanted to do was talk about it. When the crowd did leave, they often went to lunch in groups of 20. Sometimes we did not get home until 4:30 in the afternoon. Church took precedence over watching football and taking a Sunday afternoon nap.

Another change that revival brought was in how we approached worship. It soon became clear to us that a new attitude was necessary in order for us to receive the new move of God. We abandoned the passive approach—"If Jesus wants to touch me, He knows where I am"—and instead began to press in with determination to claim a fresh touch from God. Our biblical example and inspiration was the woman with the issue of blood who pushed out of the way everything that stood between her and Jesus, reached out and touched the hem of His garment, and was healed.[7]

Our music changed as well. For years we had lived on a steady diet of Hosanna-Integrity songs and charismatic classics, but the new move of God brought new songs. We not only sang new songs, we sang more songs; and the longer we sang, the stronger the anointing became.

Once we started flowing in the Holy Spirit, it was hard to stop. The signs and wonders were not merely spiritual fireworks, but demonstrations of God's power and love. God reached down from Heaven and changed the hearts of His people on the spot. Some He healed physically, others emotionally. To some He restored faith; to others, the joy of their salvation.

"Joel's Place"

One of the first undeniable signs of revival was the Sunday morning shortly after the Palm Sunday outbreak when I encountered a lady stuck to the altar rail at Communion. As I distributed

---

7.   See Mt. 9:20-22.

the wafers, I came to a curly-headed woman with a distressed look on her face.

"Have you received the bread?" I asked.

She barely managed to speak. "I can't move. I'm stuck." Her lips were drawn together and pulled down at the corners as if she were experiencing an increased gravitational force, like an astronaut during liftoff. Her right arm was hooked over the rail, and she sagged in a half-kneeling position, taking up two places.

This just will not do, I thought. *God can mess with me, He can mess with the Bible readings, and He can mess with the length of the service; but He simply cannot mess with Holy Communion!* Episcopalians pride themselves on tolerance, but I was not sure they would accept interference, even divine interference, at Communion. How could I possibly explain it to the average parishioner? *Guess who's coming to dinner? The Holy Spirit!*

Meanwhile, back at the altar rail, madame communicant continued to grimace, glued to the spot with "Holy Ghost Superglue." I searched for a quick solution. *If I lay hands on her head, maybe she will fall back under the power, and with any luck at all, will roll out of the way.* It seemed like a prudent maneuver and eased my worry about those very sweet, old ladies who were coming up the aisle to receive communion.

My plan didn't work. As I laid my hands on her head, her right arm slipped to the front, rotating her into an even worse position. Now she faced the congregation with her back pressed against the spindles of the altar rail, her body draped to the left, her arms extending like branches of a tree. Now taking up four places at the rail, she appeared to be impaled, a position she retained until 20 minutes after the service ended.

I remember thinking, *That's it, we are in serious revival. We have cut the cords of tradition and launched out into the deep. Now we are caught in a swift current, and going back is impossible.* I grinned. At this point, I would not have turned back for anything. This was Pentecost. This was that spoken of by the prophet Joel:

> *And afterward, I will pour out My Spirit on all people. Your sons and daughters will prophesy, your old men will dream dreams, your young men will see visions. Even on My servants, both men and women, I will pour out My Spirit in those days* (Joel 2:28-29).

We put the world on notice and changed the church marquee to read "Joel's Place."

A New Direction

Navigating the swift current of revival meant more than being willing to let go of tradition and liturgy; it meant launching out in a new direction. After all, our goal was never simply to break the bonds of the past, but to follow God's leading for today. If course change was difficult for the congregation, it was even more difficult for the pastor. As the captain of the ship, I was the one who had to reset the sails and rudder according to the Wind's new direction. Liturgy, once the Sunday morning destination, instead, became the jumping-off place. The question was, "Could liturgical raftriders learn to swim in the river of God?" The answer was revealed through the increased vulnerability of the pastor.

Sunday morning normally is a pastor's best opportunity to direct the sheep under his charge. The rules are simple: Be prepared, be punctual, provide good music, preach a polished pastoral sermon, minimize announcements, keep the service as short as possible, and greet visitors and members personally at the end of the service. When revival came, the Good Shepherd Himself stepped in and took over. He broke all the rules.

During the praise and worship at the beginning of each service, I knelt down as far out of sight of the congregation as I could get, praying simply, "Lord, I give this service to You. What would You have me do?" His response was always the same. He tipped

41

me over on the floor—an embarrassing pose to which I never became comfortable—and gave me a few instructions. Once, when I protested and begged the Lord not to humiliate me in front of my parishioners, He said to me, "If *you* don't yield, *they* won't yield."

Revival made me vulnerable in another way as well: I could no longer prepare in advance for the Sunday sermon. Normally, I liked to have my weekly message finished on Thursday, but now when I tried to prepare, there was no inspiration. Saturday night came—nothing; Sunday morning—nothing. My mind was blank, and my desperate prayers went unanswered. Did God close the office on the Sabbath? I was panic-stricken.

I would arrive at church, walk down the aisle, and step into the pulpit—still nothing. What was going on? Was God waiting until the last minute to see who came to church? That, at least, would be logical. Previously, some of my sharpest sermons had missed the mark because the target was absent that day (tipped off by the devil, no doubt!).

It was only when I stepped into the pulpit that the Word of Wisdom came, usually as a verse of Scripture that unfolded like a three-dimensional children's book with pop-up pages, as I spoke. Ironically, even though I had a seminary degree and 16 years of experience as a pastor, this new "impromptu" preaching was bolder than any I had ever done before. It became common for members of the congregation to remark that I seemed to be preaching directly to them. From this, I learned that the Spirit wanted me to rely upon Him every second, even in the pulpit.

Pastoral proclamation gave way to prophetic pronouncement— the velvet hammer to the sledge hammer. I heard myself saying things I could scarcely believe I was saying: scorching remarks about fruitless religion and tradition; *demanding* decisions rather than simply preaching for them. It would be reasonable to assume that this kind of preaching would run people off, but the opposite occurred. Even though some folks did leave the church, the Sunday morning attendance actually increased.

What was happening? The fire of God was melting the cold icons of our tradition and reintroducing us to a living relationship with Him that transcended religion. *Holy fire had invaded the wax museum.*

Chapter Four

Religion, Relationship, and Revival

"Those who make religion their God will not have God for their religion."

—Thomas Erskine

Viewed from the outside, Christianity is often mistaken for a philosophy or a religion. However, Christianity is not merely the wisdom of the ages, intellectual ascent to the idea of God, or a systematized set of ethical values. Christianity is, essentially, a relationship with Jesus Christ.

When the signs and wonders revival hit our church, it was like fire in a wax museum. We knew we were Episcopalians, and there was very little thought of leaving our beloved denomination. At the same time, however, the things that defined who we were, such as the Book of Common Prayer and the liturgical calendar, were no longer of principal importance. Our renewed love affair with Jesus pushed everything else to the side.

The penitential season of Lent was the first big thing to go. We tried to be solemn and gloomy and put ashes on our foreheads on Ash Wednesday, but actually we were very happy. I was so happy, in fact, that I forgot to tell Gary, our worship leader, to tone it down on the first Sunday of Lent. Gary was an outstanding keyboard player, but he had very little exposure to liturgical churches. As I put on my purple stole and tried to think about fasting and repentance, the rollicking sound of praise choruses reverberated through the sanctuary walls. *Oh no!* I thought. *We should be singing a sober hymn in a minor key, like "Forty days and forty nights, Thou was tempted in the wild." This is a time for penitence, not praise!*

I walked down the center aisle trying desperately to think of how to apologize to the congregation for this breach of musical propriety. When I reached the front of the sanctuary, however, I heard the Lord say to me, *Look at them. Listen to them.* At first, I was afraid the old-timers would be shooting darts of indignation, but that was not the case. Every hand was lifted, every voice singing, every face smiling and worshiping with vigor. It was a dream come true: a congregation who loved to worship God! Lent or no Lent, I was not about to stop them. We never quite resolved the odd sensation of feeling right and wrong at the same time—right that we were in the presence of Jesus, wrong that we were celebrating out of season—but it was all so glorious that our feelings really did not matter.

The old forms of religion were paradigms without power; they belonged to the past. Perhaps we would return to them one day, but at present, life and energy were coming from our renewed relationship with Jesus. Besides, the purpose of Lent—to cause people to examine their lives and repent of their sins—was accomplished in revival. After all, "God's kindness leads you toward repentance."[1]

---

1.   Rom. 2:4b.

Acceptable to God

By no means was everything tossed aside, nor did we ever intend to do so. In revival, some old things became new again, such as certain familiar passages of Scripture. For example, we took another look at Jesus' "job description" in the fourth chapter of Luke.

> *The Spirit of the Lord [is] upon Me, because He has anointed Me [the Anointed One, the Messiah] to preach the good news (the Gospel) to the poor; He has sent Me to announce release to the captives and recovery of sight to the blind, to send forth as delivered those who are oppressed [who are downtrodden, bruised, crushed, and broken down by calamity], to proclaim the accepted and acceptable year of the Lord [the day when salvation and the free favors of God profusely abound]* (Luke 4:18-19 AMP).

Under the fresh light of the Spirit, we realized that Jesus was anointed not to do everything, but to do five things in particular:

- Preach good news to the poor
- Announce release to the captives
- Announce recovery of sight to the blind
- Deliver the oppressed
- Proclaim the acceptable year of the Lord

Furthermore, the Spirit made it clear to us that the fresh anointing we were receiving in revival was not for our benefit alone; it was not just a "feel-good" potion for our consumption. The anointing on us was the same as that which had been on Jesus. Our divine marching orders were to walk in the anointing as Jesus did, doing the same things He had done. Revival showed us what God wanted us to do and imparted to us the Spirit and the power to do it.

A dying world needs an antidote, not an abstract philosophical truth or religious system. The anointed church, no matter how

47

small, has plenty to give: good news, release, sight, deliverance, and acceptance—practical help and the power to change lives. The gospel is the power of God for the salvation of everyone who believes: first for the Jew, then for the Gentile.[2]

What's All This About Laughing in Church?

Besides scrambling for a theological and historical understanding of revival for myself, I felt a pastoral need to explain the revival in lucid terms to a congregation who had many questions. "Where does it say anything in the Bible about laughing?" "Where does the Holy Scripture mention 'falling under the power?'"[3] "What is the purpose of signs and wonders?" "Exactly what is this thing called revival, and has anything like it happened before?" The congregation had good questions, and they deserved good answers.

Laughing Scriptures were easy to find, but it was harder to believe that similar phenomena could happen today.

> *Abraham fell facedown; he **laughed** and said to himself, "Will a son be born to a man a hundred years old? Will Sarah bear a child at the age of ninety?" ... Then God said, "Yes, but your wife Sarah will bear you a son, and you will call him Isaac [he **laughs**]"* (Genesis 17:17,19a).

> *Sarah said, "God has brought me **laughter**, and everyone who hears about this will laugh with me"* (Genesis 21:6).

> *When the Lord brought back the captives to Zion, we were like men who dreamed. Our mouths were filled with **laughter**, our tongues with songs of **joy**. Then it was said among the nations, "The Lord has done great things for them." The Lord has done great things for us, and we are filled with **joy**. Restore our*

---

2. See Rom. 1:16.
3. My favorite Scripture for falling under the power is Psalm 23:2 (KJV): "He maketh me to lie down in green pastures...."

*fortunes, O Lord, like streams in the Negev. Those who sow in tears will reap with songs of joy. He who goes out weeping, carrying seed to sow, will return with songs of **joy**, carrying sheaves with him* (Psalm 126:1-6).

*There is a time for everything, and a season for every activity under heaven: a time to be born and a time to die, a time to plant and a time to uproot, a time to kill and a time to heal, a time to tear down and a time to build, a time to weep and a time to **laugh**, a time to mourn and a time to dance* (Ecclesiastes 3:1-4).

*Looking at His disciples, He said: "Blessed are you who are poor, for yours is the kingdom of God. Blessed are you who hunger now, for you will be satisfied. Blessed are you who weep now, for you will **laugh**"* (Luke 6:20-21).

Spiritual Fallout?

The joy and laughter we experienced in church could not be contained, and even though we knew it offended some in the congregation, we sensed it was from the Spirit of God and completely consistent with the Word of God. On the other hand, the falling phenomenon, although common in revival history, was harder to find in Scripture. In our church, people usually, although not always, fell backward. In the Bible, in what could be interpreted as acts of veneration, most of the people fell face forward. Yet there were notable exceptions.

*...then the house was filled with a cloud, even the house of the Lord; so that the priests **could not stand** to minister by reason of the cloud: for the glory of the Lord had filled the house of God* (2 Chronicles 5:13-14 KJV).

This had been my experience on Palm Sunday. When the glory of the Lord fell, I was immobilized, unable to continue with the service. I could not stand because something like a weight pressed down on me, forcing me to the ground. It was an involuntary action similar to Paul's response on the road to Damascus.

> *As he neared Damascus on his journey, suddenly a light from heaven flashed around him. He **fell** to the ground and heard a voice say to him, "Saul, Saul, why do you persecute Me?"* (Acts 9:3-4)

The popular term for Christians falling to the ground, "slain in the Spirit," is a descriptive term rather than a biblical term. It implies a similarity to St. John's experience in the Revelation when he encountered "someone 'like a son of man.' "[4] The "someone" was the glorified Christ.

> *In His right hand He held seven stars, and out of His mouth came a sharp double-edged sword. His face was like the sun shining in all its brilliance. When I saw Him, I fell at His feet as though dead* (Revelation 1:16-17a).

In our church, people fell to the ground most frequently when they came forward for ministry and received the laying on of hands. At other times, falling was associated with the proclamation of the Word, as in my case when I read the Gospel on Palm Sunday. I explained the phenomenon as an overwhelming personal encounter with the glory of God. Some people readily accepted this explanation, while others shook their heads as a sign not so much of doubt, but of the fact that they simply could not comprehend it.

How Do You Explain Revival?

Trying to "comprehend" a mystery of God may have been the problem. Still, we felt obligated to teach people about the manifestations of the Spirit. Testimonies from Church history seemed to help.

---

4.   See Rev. 1:13.

John Wesley's *Journal* tells of people who during his preaching "were stuck to the ground and lay there groaning."[5]

The preaching of the Methodist circuit-rider Peter Cartwright was also accompanied by listeners falling under the power. Similar results accompanied George Whitefield's preaching and are attested in the writings of Jonathan Edwards as well.[6]

Charles G. Finney's *Autobiography* recounts episodes in which people could not move or speak, in one instance for 16 hours.[7]

Sixteen hours? That sounded incredible until we witnessed for ourselves a woman at one of the revival meetings we held later in Gainesville, Florida who fell out under the power for *18* hours!

Some sheep chose not to follow no matter how logical the explanations were. Others followed but dragged their feet. Still others followed eagerly, as evidenced by the joyful expression on their faces. As the revival continued in the weeks that followed, tension mounted between those who wanted the deeper things of God and those who thought we were headed in the wrong direction. In 18 years of ordained ministry, I had never felt the tension of leadership so strongly. Revival brought a focus to the congregation, yet at the same time, scattered some sheep to every point on the compass.

No Compromise

More than once, I thought of quitting. Why not give in to the grumblers and head back to "Egypt" as the rebellious Israelites in the wilderness wanted to do? Yet I knew that would be a costly decision. If I pulled back, the majority of the congregation, who were going with the flow, would be disappointed. Many would leave to find a church that was running with revival fire, and who could have blamed them? On the other hand, if I kept flowing with the river of God, there would be more and more pastoral challenges.

---

5. Knox, 1950, 472, citing Wesley's Journal, p. 118.
6. *Ibid*, 526, 529, 530.
7. Wesley, 1977, reprint, 58.

Could there be a compromise? A half-revived church with a lukewarm relationship with Jesus? Absolutely not! Leaders do not compromise on major issues. A "Pontius Pilate" pleases the crowd; a "Paul," a "Silas," or a "Timothy" pleases God.[8]

What About the Bishop?

One question I was often asked after the revival began was, "What does your bishop think about you?" The question implied that the person who asked it expected a negative response. I understood their suspicion. One old prelate told me he abhorred three things: biblical fundamentalism, the "Order of the Silly Grin" (Spirit-filled people who smiled all the time), and those who told him, "I can see the Holy Spirit in you." Many bishops are proudly anti-charismatic.

My bishop was not like that, but I knew that I better keep him informed about all the changes in the parish. One Tuesday morning Fran and I visited The Right Reverend John W. Howe, the Bishop of Central Florida. He greeted us warmly as we entered his Orlando office. Although he was baptized in the Holy Spirit and familiar with charismatic ministry, I was somewhat nervous as to what his reaction might be.

After we chatted a few minutes, I told him about how revival had affected the congregation, focusing on the changed lives and the fruit the Spirit was producing. He was very receptive and happy to hear the good news. He prayed with us and blessed us. I left encouraged and thankful to have such a discerning overseer. He was an assuring landmark as I sailed through uncharted waters.

God Called the Shots

One significant consequence of the revival and my deepened relationship with Jesus was that for the first time in almost 20 years of ministry, I had no vision. My confidence in the Lord was never

---

8.   "We are not trying to please men but God..." (1 Thess. 2:4b).

stronger, but I honestly had no idea where this move of God was headed. The further along I went and the deeper into the river I plunged, the more I discovered that many other pastors on the cutting edge of revival were having the same experience. One pastor from Chicago told me that before Rodney Howard-Browne came to his church, the pastor told his congregation, "If you ask me questions during the revival, I will give you one of three answers: 'I don't know,' 'I don't care,' or 'It doesn't matter.' "

Far from giving an indifferent response, he was simply being honest. Pastors are used to having vision, a direction in which to lead the flock, but when revival came, God took the lead. It was like being on a bus tour where the itinerary, the food, and the lodging were all prearranged. All we had to do was show up on time and leave the driving to God. Revival pastors learned to step back so the sheep could have a closer walk with the Shepherd. When pastors moved out of the way, parishioners felt free to step forward in ministry.

This happened more and more in my own congregation. Elaine, one of our members, stopped me after church one Sunday to tell me about another member who was entering the Lakeland Regional Hospital. "Now don't worry about a thing," she assured me. "Lou [her husband] and I are going to drive him to the hospital and sit with his wife during the procedure. We will make sure she is taken care of and that people are praying for him. You can drop by if you want to, but it is really not necessary. Everyone knows that you don't like to go to the hospital."

It was true. The only reason I visited the sick was because I vowed to do it when I was ordained and because people expected it. I acknowledged that it should be done, but I loathed going to hospitals. I abhorred their smells and felt queasy at the sight of blood. Once, when visiting a sick judge at my first parish in Jacksonville, Florida, I passed out cold and ended up in the emergency room. Some pastors loved to pray for their parishioners before their 5:00 a.m. surgeries, but not me.

53

Lou was a diabetic and Elaine was used to trips to the emergency room. They both had a burning love for the Lord in their hearts, and when the opportunity came to serve Him in the pastoral ministry, they were naturals. Not only did they do a much better job than I could have, but they enjoyed doing it. Revival brought out the best in people.

From Burned-out to Recharged

Increased involvement from the congregation was not the only benefit for the pastors. A cardinal sign of revival was the pastor's own refreshment. Heavy burdens, heartaches, and the pain of rejections were lifted from clergy and their spouses. The Good Shepherd assumed the care of the cleric as well as the congregation. Professional ministers were rejuvenated in their own relationship with Jesus.

At the Lakeland Revival, Fran and I went forward every time Rodney Howard-Browne offered prayers for pastors and their spouses. Hundreds came forward and stood in long lines on the vast platform waiting expectantly for a drink of the "new wine." We all had something in common: Ten, 20, 30, or 40 years ago, we had all taken up the call to the ordained ministry with aspirations of changing the world for Jesus, only to discover that the world was not eager to be changed and neither, for that matter, was the Church.

In the days that followed, many of the pastors who came for prayer shared their testimonies. They were surprisingly similar. "I was burned-out. Now I am charged up and ready to go." "We were ready to quit," one woman in her 30's reported, "but the Lord restored us and filled us with fresh oil. We are excited about what He is going to do in our congregation."

After my own refreshment, I was confident that God was in control of the church, which was fine with me. He did not tell me His plans for the future so when someone asked, "What's going on in the parish?" I simply said, "It's revival." That answer was sufficient for me, but the average churchman wanted to know where all this was leading. It was a question that I could not answer. "I feel like the captain of a sailboat caught in a hurricane," I said, "hanging onto the mast, trying not to be washed overboard. I have no idea where the Wind is taking the ship."

Although I knew the answer was a bit off-putting, I enjoyed it. After years of church management and leadership seminars that taught me "how to do church," it was nice to have time off. Since it was impossible to manage the big waves of the renewal hurricane anyway, I decided to enjoy the ride. I went to church on Sunday not to persuade people, but simply to see what the Lord would do next. What use to be toil was now a pleasure.

For the first time, I discovered what it was like to have God direct the order of service. In some churches, the sheep are in control. Others are controlled by the pastor. When revival came, it was as if Heaven opened and the hand of God reached down to manage things directly. On Sunday, all I had to do was ask Him what was on the menu for the day and then serve it up to the congregation. Of course, the congregation still looked to the pastor for leadership, but I no longer felt like I was pushing a flock of sheep uphill. The method seemed like holy chaos, but out of the chaos a new creation was formed.

That new creation was a congregation who had less religion and more relationship with Jesus and with one another. That revived relationship with Jesus produced the fruit of the Holy Spirit in great abundance.

Chapter Five

Where's the Fruit?

In many ways, revival caught us completely by surprise, ushering in a renewed relationship with Jesus that we scarcely realized we needed, and effecting changes that were completely unexpected. Although we knew very little about true revival and the changes it brings, we learned quickly. Our members crisscrossed concordances looking for biblical references to the words *joy* and *laugh*. We read everything we could find on revival and reread Scripture passages about signs and wonders. Caught up in a swift-moving current, we scrambled to get our bearings. Question after question arose as we tried to understand what was happening and to explain it to people who had not experienced it. Inquiring minds wanted to know, and one question seemed to surface more often than any other: "Where is the fruit?"

More often than not, the "fruit question" came from the non-revived. Historically, those who study revival (rather than experience it) are most apt to try to measure its genuineness by the type and amount of "spiritual fruit" that results. Usually, however, they are not referring to the fruit of "love, joy, peace, patience, kindness, goodness, faithfulness, gentleness, and self-control."[1] Instead, the question "Where's the fruit?" actually means, "What are the tangible benefits of this revival?" What they are really looking for is evidence of a harvest of souls or of moral changes in society as proof of genuine revival.

For the revived, experience was proof enough. The joy that broke out in the form of laughter and permeated almost every church service was positively the fruit of the Spirit. When the unseen hand of God touched me, I knew beyond doubt who it was. My spirit discerned the presence of the Holy Spirit, but there was concrete evidence of genuine revival as well.

Indeed, we saw many souls won to Christ, but the work that God did in the hearts of believers was even more impressive. Well-meaning Christians put the cart before the horse when they look for a soul harvest as the *first* fruit of revival. What they fail to realize is that true revival always begins inside the Church, stirring up faith, recovering lost sheep, and calling for repentance. G. Campbell Morgan said, "Revival is the reanimation of the life of the believer (not the unregenerate as they are 'dead in sin')...there can only be revival where there is life to revive."[2] Revival is not for the lost, but for the Church. The lost are dead in their sins and need to be reborn, not revived. Evangelism, on the other hand, is a natural by-product of a church that is on fire for Jesus.

Smoking or Non-smoking?

Before revival came to our parish, bringing people to Jesus was a tedious and exasperating effort, with much sowing and little harvest. With the fresh anointing, giving an altar call was almost as easy as saying, "Smoking or 'non'?" I desperately wanted my congregation to be evangelistic—to tell people about Jesus and to

---

1.   See Gal 5:22-23.

2.   Selwyn Hughes, *Revival: Times of Refreshing* (Sunburry-on-Thames, Middlesex: CWR, 1990), 12.

bring them to church. We tried every evangelism program that
came down the pike, but they were all unsuccessful. Prevailing wisdom said that church programs were the way to attract newcomers, and there was no lack of vendors hawking their wears:
"Programs! Programs! Get your church programs." It was almost
as if Jesus had said, "Go ye into all the world and program the
gospel."

We tried James Kennedy's "Evangelism Explosion," the
"Happy Hunter's Take Your City for Jesus," the Diocesan Cathedral's "Take a Loaf of Fresh Bread to the Visitors" program, and
direct mailing to new residents within a 50-mile radius of the
church. While these programs may have worked for others, they
did not work for us. Evangelism Explosion produced as many
quarrels as conversions. Our 25 Happy Hunter neighborhood canvassing teams won only two people to Christ, and those two never
came to the church. The "fresh bread" program quickly grew stale
and soon deteriorated to the point of handing visitors a frozen loaf
of bread along with their church bulletin as they entered the
church. If they held a Prayer Book in one hand and a hymnal in
the other, the only place for the frozen loaf was between their
knees. It gave new meaning to the term "the frozen chosen."

The direct mailing campaign was our own idea. We purchased
mailing labels from a marketing firm and printed picture postcards. The front of the card had a photograph of a glass of wine
next to a baguette of French bread. The text read, "Jesus of
Nazareth invites you to a dinner given in His honor." This sounded so-o-o Episcopal, and we were sure it would cause the church,
at minimum, to double in size. We sent out 7,000 cards—and
received three responses. Two of these were from women who
phoned to say how very upset they were to receive a church card
addressed to their late husbands. *Great,* I thought, *now we're doing*
negative *evangelism.*

So much for church programs! Why do we need them anyway? Should not the Church of Jesus Christ stand on its own merit? If we have something real to offer, why do we connive and contrive schemes to lure people with food that is not real food?[3] Revival renews the Church's relationship with the Person of the Holy Spirit, and it is He who produces good fruit.

Altar Calls

One of the first "fruits" of revival that was particularly delicious was that evangelism became natural and spontaneous. From the outset, members of our congregation brought friends to church not to hear the preacher or for the annual picnic, but because they were excited about what *God* was doing. Every Sunday there were signs, wonders, and miracles, and a floor covered with people lying peacefully in the Spirit. Our members reached out to their friends and shared the blessing.

Week after week, visitors came to our church to experience the power of God. One man who attended our church arrived half an hour late on his first visit. Later, he described what happened to him.

"When I opened the door to the sanctuary, the power and presence of God hit me. I could barely walk down the aisle to find a seat. I saw a cloud looming over the front of the sanctuary. When I came forward to receive communion, I walked into the cloud as I approached the altar rail."

Although he was the only one who saw the cloud of glory that day, what happened next was even more unusual. As he tried to walk through the cloud, he was suddenly flung backward as if he had run into an obstruction and bounced off. His arms flew out from his sides as he crashed to the floor. He looked like "Wile E. Coyote" from the "Roadrunner" cartoons after he has slammed into a canyon wall. His entire body reverberated as he recoiled from the invisible cloud. His eyes rolled back into his head, and his

---

3.   See Jn. 6:55.

mouth hung open. He was not injured, and after his encounter with the cloud, drifted off in the Spirit for more than 30 minutes. No one knew what happened to him, and no harm was done, except for the inconvenience of having to step over his body on the way to communion. As the revival wore on, supernatural encounters such as this became normal, especially for visitors.

One of the early fruits of revival in my own life was a commitment to the use of altar calls in the worship service. The Episcopal Church is not known for giving altar calls, but I was brought face-to-face with their effectiveness during the Lakeland Revival. Rodney Howard-Browne issued an altar call every night as the Spirit led—not always at the same point in the service. On some occasions, he even issued the call *before* the sermon. Regardless of when they were given, the altar calls always brought a phenomenal response. Usually, hundreds came forward; on one particular night, over 500 people stood at the front. They came to receive salvation or assurance, or to "rededicate" their lives to the Lord. "Rededication" meant repentance. Thousands of wayward Christians, lost sheep who had strayed away from the Lord, returned to the fold.

Why is it that churches with altars rarely have altar calls, while churches without altars have them all the time? It is because mainline traditional churches take one of three views. Some assume that everyone at Sunday worship has the gift of eternal life by virtue of their baptism; altar calls are therefore superfluous. Others view salvation as an internal working of God's grace, making public commitment an unnecessary work. Still others, overtly or covertly, teach universalism—that *everyone* will be saved and go to Heaven—so why bother with an altar call?

Any hesitation or objections I may have had initially to the altar calls were washed away as I watched tears of repentance stream down the faces of those who were deeply touched by the love of God. How could I object as I witnessed hundreds of people receive salvation and have their lives radically changed by the

Lord? After all, they were experiencing the same thing that had happened to me years before when I received Jesus while alone in my car. In fact, initially my main reason for going into the ministry had been to bring people to Jesus. The altar call forced me to face the question of what had taken away my zeal to see sinners saved.

How much time had I wasted playing church? How many souls had been lost because evangelism was not important in Episcopal tradition? I remembered my first four years as a priest and youth minister—only one person was saved. Why was it so easy to be content with lukewarm religion? By contrast, I was thrilled every day at the revival meetings by salvations, healings, and testimonies of changed lives. After a few weeks, I knew I could not go back to church as usual. I resolved to give altar calls and bring people to Jesus myself. That decision changed my life, my ministry, and my church.

Drawn by the Spirit

In some ways, the scene at our church after revival hit looked a little bizarre, but it was not off-putting to the visitors as some feared it would be. On the contrary, most were intrigued. People invited their friends more often instead of less. As word spread, others came on their own. We did not plan, push, or program it, but somehow evangelism became the natural work of the church.

Shortly after the revival began, my family went on a long-planned vacation trip to New England. The revival continued without us. After returning home several weeks later, I observed a number of people I had never seen before roaming the halls of the church. When I asked one young woman how long she had been coming, she responded, "Three weeks. Who are you?"

As it turned out, her name was Glenda and the circumstances of her coming to the church were unusual. For one entire Saturday evening she had been unable to sleep because God had repeatedly shown her a picture of Christ the King Episcopal Church and told her she must attend church there the next day. Her husband was an alcoholic who had recently stopped drinking, but was what some call a "dry drunk," one who had stopped drinking but still craved alcohol. He refused to come with her Sunday, but agreed to attend the Wednesday evening Bible study.

Glenda's husband, a former Roman Catholic, came forward when prayer was offered, expecting to receive the traditional ecclesiastical blessing, where the sign of the cross is traced on the forehead with the priest's thumb. Suddenly, however, he was thrown to the floor where he lay unconscious for 15 or 20 minutes, occasionally rolling back and forth with a groan. After he came to his senses, he found that he had been completely delivered from alcoholism, and all desire to take a drink was gone. He also received Jesus and the in-filling of the Holy Spirit.

This was typical of the new evangelism. Relationships with Jesus were initiated and rekindled in the midst of healings and miracles. It was not a new evangelism program. It was simply the "fruit" of revival.

The Lawd Said, "UH-HUH"

One evening at the Lakeland Revival, Brother Glover approached me before the meeting began. Every regular member of Carpenter's knew Brother Glover because he shouted "Glory!" loud enough to be heard in every corner of the 10,000-seat auditorium. In his own words, he described himself as "just an ignorant black man that God called to preach the gospel."

"The Lawd done told me," he began, "that I was gwine to preach in yo' church, and that you was gonna take up an offerin' fo' me so I could buy a Greyhound bus and go minister to the drug addicts in New Yo'k City."

Preach in my congregation? Not likely, I thought. *Was someone with a sixth-grade education going to assume the pulpit of the church of the Presidents?* But just in case, I prayed about it. "Lord, You don't want me to invite Brother Glover to our congregation, do You?"

Uh-huh!

"But Lord!" I protested.

Uh-huh! Invite him!

"But..." *Oh, never mind.* I gulped. "Why, Brother Glover, that would be just fine."

Brother Glover preached at both the eight and the ten o'clock services two weeks after "the Lawd said, 'Uh-huh.' " This was Glover's first time with "Piscapedians," as he called us. He gave his testimony and talked about his reluctance to preach with a limited education. "But the Lawd told me not to worry. He said He would tell me what to say, and He do, too!"

Brother Glover told us about his ministry in "the bottoms," a poor section of town that was a crossroads of prostitutes and drug traffickers. He knocked on doors and asked people if they knew Jesus. If they did not, he told them about the Lord and invited them to his church.

When he came to our church, Brother Glover brought his music ministry team with him. His pianist and the rest of the band turned the place upside down, and we broke into a new realm of worship. Many of us found a new freedom: a freedom to dance, a freedom to shout, a freedom to move about.

The church also broke into a new realm of giving. Sure enough, the offering for Brother Glover was enough to make a down payment on a used Greyhound—more than a thousand dollars. William, a member of the church, had set aside enough money to pay the rent on his business the following week, but instead gave it to Brother Glover. He did not know how he was going to meet his financial obligations, but said the Lord told him to do it. That very week his business was better than usual, and several customers who owed money dropped by and paid him. By the end of the week, William had enough to pay his rent and a surplus.

Brother Glover was a good example of obedience, giving, and blessing. He obeyed the leading of the Lord, we followed suit, the congregation was set free, and William was blessed with money to spare. It was typical chain-reaction godly giving, a typical "fruit" of revival.

Attitude Adjustment

Money is a four-letter word in most churches and is rarely mentioned per se. Pastors skirt the issue with words like *stewardship*, *finances*, *funds*, and *treasure*. It is acceptable to mention *tithes*, *offerings*, and *alms*, but not *M-O-N-E-Y*. Revival exposed a horrible sin in the Body of Christ—unfaithfulness in giving. I tried never to overestimate my congregation's knowledge or underestimate their ability to learn, but I missed it on the issue of money. It was time for an attitude adjustment.

That adjustment, like most of the revival innovations, began with me. Previously, I would instruct Fran to lock her purse in the trunk whenever we visited Carpenter's Home Church. "Those Pentecostals will preach every dime out of your pocket," I told her. I was a reluctant giver—one with a wrong attitude.

Before the Lakeland Revival, any offering I gave at Carpenter's was calculated according to a formula. I took the cost of opening up the church, which I knew to be $10,000, and divided it by the number of people present—say 2,000. That came to a cost of $5 per person, which I doubled to cover those who gave nothing. To that $10 I added $5 for the guest preacher and another $5 "just to bless them." That totaled $20. I reasoned that $20 was a fair offering because taking my family to the movies for the evening would have cost more than that.

Revival changed my attitude about giving. I learned to give based on the Word of God. Fran and I had been tithers for years, but now we learned to be givers. The Bible says we should give generously,[4] willingly,[5] and cheerfully.[6] That is the right attitude. The Bible also says to sow, that is, to give in expectation that you will reap generously.[7] We began to notice that the Bible had a lot to say about money. As we taught the people about God's financial plan, they became cheerful givers as well, and the church had what it needed for the ministry. For the first time, our congregation finished the year with a surplus. Our prosperity confounded the critics, and we laughed all the way to the bank.

Prayers Answered

Another "fruit" of revival came from answered prayers. As the intensity of the anointing increased, our faith increased, and as our faith increased, we saw more prayers answered. Nothing increases faith like seeing firsthand the intervention of God in present circumstances. We began to pray with the expectation that God would answer.

A modern aphorism says, "If you can't run with the big dogs, stay on the porch." Our congregation decided to run with the big dogs and purchased a sophisticated audio system—so sophisticated, in fact, that no one knew how to make it work properly. We needed a knowledgeable audio technician to run the soundboard.

Volunteers sounded like the logical solution, so we advertised for help. Two men signed up. One could not hear high frequencies, and the other wore a hearing aid in each ear. The spirit was

---

4. "...if it is contributing to the needs of others, let him give generously" (Rom. 12:8a).

5. "For if the willingness is there, the gift is acceptable according to what one has..." (2 Cor. 8:12).

6. "Remember this: Whoever sows sparingly will also reap sparingly, and whoever sows generously will also reap generously. Each man should give what he has decided in his heart to give, not reluctantly or under compulsion, for God loves a cheerful giver" (2 Cor. 9:6-7).

7. Ibid.

willing, but the flesh was weak. Someone in the congregation then had a radical thought. "Why don't we ask God to send someone?"

The very next Sunday I asked the congregation to pray for a qualified sound person. Following the service, two visitors, both audio technicians, approached me. One of them, whose name was Paul, had recently resigned from another church after crossing wires with his boss. He needed a place to lick his wounds, and we needed his expertise. Before the revival, I would have shied away from hiring someone without a sterling set of references, but afterward, I relied more on the grace of God to change lives. Paul was an answer to prayer and proved to be fully capable of exorcising the sophisticated electronic demons in the soundboard.

A Healing Miracle

Priscilla was nearly 80 and a bit stooped over from osteoporosis. She and her husband were regular, active members of our church. Although the prayer line had become an essential part of every service, Priscilla had always been reluctant to come forward. Following the service one Sunday morning, however, another member approached me on her behalf and told me that Priscilla wanted prayer.

"Bring her here immediately," I said. This was a major departure from what I had been taught during the charismatic renewal. The common belief was that the anointing was present only during the service. When the service was over, the anointing lifted. It was plausible reasoning in light of the Scripture that said, "The power of the Lord was present for Him to heal the sick."[8] This would explain why evangelists who entered a hospital could not heal everyone; the anointing was not always present.

Revival changed my way of thinking. My instruction to bring Priscilla in immediately was a new reaction: impromptu, spontaneous, and more like the way Jesus responded. Can you imagine

---

8.　Lk. 5:17b.

Jesus telling someone, "I'm sorry, but the anointing has lifted. Please come back next week"?

When Priscilla reentered the sanctuary, I took her hand and led her to the front. I was so used to seeing her stooped over that I assumed she wanted prayer for something other than her back, but I was wrong. Her back hurt and she wanted help. The time for faith had come. Praying for an "incurable" condition such as osteoporosis often raises reasonable doubts in one's mind. However, fear often masquerades as reasonable doubt, while "faith is being sure of what we hope for and certain of what we do not see."[9] I prayed in faith.

I called for one of our laymen to stand behind Priscilla as a catcher. Priscilla assured me that would not be necessary. "I've never been 'slain in the Spirit.' " That may have been true, but revival had a way of changing things. As soon as I laid hands upon Priscilla, she gently fell backward onto the bright red carpet. Because her spine was bent at the neck, her head was six inches off the floor when she was lying on her back. Two prayer books and a hymnal stacked together provided a perfect headrest.

In the weeks that followed, Priscilla gradually improved. Her pain was reduced substantially, and her neck eventually straightened to the point where she needed only two prayer books, then one, then none! From then on, Priscilla was the first one in line for prayer every Sunday; it did not matter what we were praying for. Her son, a clergyman who was skeptical and antagonistic about charismatic ministry, wrote to say that he had reversed his opinion. Priscilla became a walking, talking testimony to her family and friends.

Personal Fruit

One of the best illustrations of the effects of revival is the fruit that it bore in me personally. Revival changed my life, my marriage, and my family relationships. My children noticed the change

---

9.   Heb. 11:1.

right away. The tennis shoe dilemma is a good example. Before the revival, I often came home and greeted my children with "Whose shoes are these in the middle of the floor? How many times have I told you not to leave your tennis shoes in the living room? Come and get them right now!" I knew it was a rude way to enter the room and I usually regretted it, but I couldn't seem to stop doing it. I feared that my children would grow up remembering their father as an overbearing, tyrannical, growling bear.

Revival did not change the tennis shoe dilemma, but it changed me. The shoes continued to clutter the living room, but my attitude and behavior were different. *I must be in the right house*, I joked to myself. Now, I greeted my children with "Daddy's home! Tell me about your day!" I am thankful beyond words for Elizabeth and Hugh. One day all too soon they will be gone to college or down the aisle to be married, or perhaps carrying the gospel to a foreign land. I will miss them one day, but today I'm glad they're here.

Jim Taylor, a priest from the south end of Lakeland with whom I played tennis every Thursday morning, also noticed the change in me. "I was worried about you," he said. "You were really letting stress and anger get the best of you. But now, you are full of the joy of the Lord." Even my tennis game improved, but not enough to beat Father Taylor.

Revival gave me a brand-new heart, one that was full of compassion for my church. It was not counterfeit religion or pure emotionalism, but the real thing. Most of the transformations were on the inside, but they were observable on the outside.

One of our retired church members commented, "Our fellowship group had a prophecy 12 months ago, that we would have a new pastor within a year. It puzzled us because we could not figure out how it could happen. The prophecy has come true. We do have a new pastor—it is you. We see a new compassion when you pray for people."

Me, compassionate? That was a first. No one had ever called me compassionate. I knew my spiritual gifts, and compassion was not one of them. I was not cold or indifferent, just sometimes oblivious to people's feelings. After my fresh touch from Heaven, I began to see people as Jesus did. Looking past outward appearances, I saw straight into their hearts. Sensing people's hurt moved me to pray for them. It was a change for the better, the result of the Spirit's work inside.

A revived relationship with my wife, Fran, was a delightful and unexpected fruit. Our marriage was not on the rocks, but it had degenerated to roles with various delegated duties: "You take out the trash, and I'll do the soccer run." I was content with the status quo, but unknown to me, I was driving my wife crazy.

At least once a month, so I learned, Fran locked herself in her prayer closet (the bathroom), faced east (the only practical way one could face in our east-west running bathroom), and knelt down on the oriental prayer carpet (the bathroom rug from Taiwan), where she beseeched the Almighty with the "Wife's Prayer": "God, You made him! God, You saved him! Now, God, You fix him!"

During the revival, Fran learned a new prayer: "God, change me," referring to herself. It was a concept she had never thought of before. Her prayers changed from "God, change him" to "God, change me." The new prayer yielded three benefits: She changed, I changed, and our relationship changed—all for the better. She even looked different. I saw my wife of 20 years as I had when we first started dating: beautiful inside and out.

The biggest reformation of all was in my relationship with Jesus. Although I believed intellectually that Christianity was a relationship with Christ rather than a religion, I had not maintained that relationship very well. Functionally, I had become just another company employee with a job to do. I did not spend much time sitting at the feet of the Boss. Once revival came, my devotional life was transformed. Bible reading and study took on a new life and importance. My prayer life increased as well, but now, instead of intercession and petition, I spent more time offering myself to God, simply sitting in God's presence and basking in the anointing of the Holy Spirit. This became a daily occurrence that usually lasted 30 minutes or more.

True revival must be more than signs and wonders; it must touch and change our most intimate relationships!

The Heart of Revival

One evening at the Lakeland Revival, Rodney Howard-Browne asked me and a dozen other pastors to follow him as he prayed for the evening crowd of 7,000 people. Our specific instructions were to linger and pray for those who did not fall under the Spirit—those who needed a breakthrough or intensive prayer for deliverance.

I came to a young woman standing alone in a long line where everyone else had fallen to the floor. She must have wondered, as did I, why she was the only one who had not fallen. I laid my hand on her head and began to pray in the Spirit. Her head bowed a little, but there was no other response. She was rigid, seemingly caught up in her own thoughts.

Suddenly, a voice inside me said, *Give her a hug.* What? Hug a stranger? I resisted the thought as visions of sexual harassment charges danced in my head. *Give her a hug,* the voice insisted. The woman's husband, who was standing behind her as her catcher, was built like a weight lifter—a *very* good reason not to hug her, I thought. The voice became demanding. *I said, give her a hug! Hug her now!*

"Ur, um, excuse me," I said timidly. "I believe the Lord wants me to give you a hug. Is that all right with you?"

Without looking up, she nodded. So did her husband. *Whew!*

71

Stretching out my arms, I embraced her gently but somewhat stiffly. Still uncomfortable with the idea and not knowing what else to do, I prayed softly in the Spirit. The woman did not sob or make a sound as a steady stream of tears ran down her cheeks. After a minute or two, she lifted her head, and I saw her face for the first time.

"Thank you," she said. "I came tonight with one request of God. I asked Him that if He still loved me, to reach out in some way and touch me. You see, I am HIV positive; I have AIDS. I know I've made a lot of mistakes in my life, but I needed to know that no matter what, God still loves me."

Her words were burned into my memory. Who doesn't need to know that? She needed gentleness, not judgment. She needed the "tender mercy of our God."[10] I never saw the woman or her husband again, but I know that she received what she came for—the assurance of God's love. I received something as well, the *raison d'être* for revival: People everywhere, even church people, need to be assured of the love of Jesus. What greater "fruit" of revival could there be than that?

---

10. See Lk. 1:78.

Chapter
Six

Feeding the Sheep

Religion that God our Father accepts as pure and faultless is this: to look after orphans and widows in their distress... (James 1:27).

One of the biggest blessings that came with revival was the Anchor House for boys. Twenty years earlier, Mark Rivera had pioneered a ministry for runaways and "throwaways." Since its beginning, 2,000 young men had been given a chance to rebuild their lives at "Pop" Rivera's Anchor House. Mark and 20 teenage boys joined our church shortly after the revival began.

The Anchor House boys were eager to receive a touch from the Lord, which made them different from most of our other teenagers, as well as many regular church members. They illustrated what Jesus meant when He said, "Anyone who will not receive the kingdom of God like a little child will never enter it."[1] Every time we offered prayer, they came. Some were typically

---

1.   Mk. 10:15b.

reluctant adolescents, but most needed no coaxing whatsoever. Abused sexually, physically, verbally, their darkened lives were drawn to the brightly burning light of Jesus. They needed help, and they knew it.

Week after week the call was given, "If you need a touch from God this morning, please come forward. I want to pray for you." One by one these boys and young men slowly stood, slipped out of their rows, and came to the altar rail where I instructed them, "Lift your hands, close your eyes, and simply receive from the Lord." With heads slightly bowed, they collapsed into the waiting arms of men of the church who stood behind them and lowered them to the floor.

Like the woman with the issue of blood in the eighth chapter of Luke who pressed forward to Jesus for healing, the Anchor House boys recognized the necessity of divine help in their lives and knew where to get it. Some of them were from Christian homes and were versed in Scripture, but most were not. Yet, they all knew their troubled condition and sensed that something good and comforting emanated from our church. These boys, of their own volition, reached out to receive the power of God to change their lives.

Most of the boys were bashful when it came to talking about their experiences, but the inward change was visible on the outside in many ways, especially in their haircuts. The new boys were fresh off the street and often sported shaved heads or asymmetrical or punk rock haircuts as a symbol of their rebellion. Over the course of a few weeks or months, their hairstyles became more conventional, and life began to fill their cloudy, dull eyes.

Turning Up the Heat

One morning as I knelt for prayer at the beginning of the service, the Lord directed me to extend an altar call, but I resisted. *Give the invitation*, He insisted. I acknowledged the request, but did nothing. A third command finally persuaded me to stand and offer a chance for people to receive Jesus, but I wondered at the Lord's insistence.

At first, no one came. I repeated the invitation; still no one responded. God had told me in no uncertain terms to do it. Why were there no results? I was puzzled. Then I realized that the empty altar rail was not my problem. It was the Counselor's job to convict the world of sin.[2] If He wanted people to come forward, He could draw them. It was a moment of revelation.

"I am very sorry to have to do this," I said, improvising with the new insight. "The Lord told me to give this invitation, and now I must ask Him to turn up the heat so that those who are supposed to be up here will come forward. Soon, some of you will start to feel warm as the fire of the Spirit convicts you and draws you to Jesus." The reaction was sudden and dramatic. Three teenage boys sprang from their seats and ran forward.

Somehow I knew that this was not all. "There are more of you," I announced. Two more came forward from the back of the church. Now there were five, but I sensed that someone was still missing.

A sixth boy had folded the Sunday bulletin into pleats and was fanning himself vigorously. Danny was a fifteen-year-old whom a judge had sentenced to the Anchor House after a year in juvenile detention for killing a 19-month-old girl. "It's hot in here," he gasped.

"No," I said. "The Holy Spirit is calling you." A faithful couple from the parish who were sitting next to him urged him to go forward. The service came to a standstill for five or ten minutes while Danny made up his mind. The other five teens waited patiently at the front. The rest of the congregation craned their necks in an attempt to witness this unfolding drama of redemption.

---

2.   See Jn. 16:7-8.

That morning six teenage boys received Jesus. *Finally*, I thought, *the Church is being the Church: anointed by the Spirit, sent by the Father to those Jesus came to save!*

Little Guy

The boys of the Anchor House were eager for a touch from God, but God was even more eager to touch them. One Thursday, I ministered at the Anchor House's evening service. As the boys began to fall under the power, I noticed one little guy in particular who fell, scrambled to his feet, and stood in line again four times in a row. I wondered, was he hungry for God or just playing?

As it turned out, "Little Guy" had a very *big* need. During refreshments afterward, he sat beside me on the sofa in the living room. Experience in prison ministry had taught me not to probe, but the Lord prompted me to ask Little Guy a question.

"Where is your mother?"

"I don't know. I don't remember her. She left when I was two years old, and no one knows where she is."

"What about your dad? Where is he?"

"He's in prison."

"Why is your dad in prison?"

"For sexually abusing me."

In an instant, I saw why God sent the fresh anointing to His Church. We needed supernatural power to minister to Little Guy and thousands more like him. No amount of counseling could put his life together again; no amount of money or social programs could restore what he had lost. Jesus, on the other hand, was anointed to bind up the brokenhearted. He is the One who can put shattered lives back together again.

As our congregation moved deeper into the Spirit, we began to see deeper into the needs of the human soul, needs that could only be met by the power of the Holy Spirit. Simply put, the revival brought a fresh anointing to continue the work of Jesus, the Anointed One.

Tough Guy

Another young man was touched at Anchor House that night. He was the opposite of Little Guy—strong, tough, and well built. When I arrived for the service that evening, "Tough Guy" was competing with another boy in a push-up contest. Tough Guy was the top dog, the house leader, the one most feared and revered.

When it was prayer time, Tough Guy stayed away. Several boys tried to get him to come forward, but he shook his head and continued to stare at the floor. The Lord spoke to me. *Pray for him.*

Extending my arm, I offered to shake hands with the tough and tense young man. He only shook his head sternly and cast his eyes downward. *Pray for him*, the voice commanded, but I was reluctant. Tough Guy had the same "I'm okay, leave me alone" mentality that some of the adults in my church displayed. The Lord wanted to touch him, but Tough Guy was unwilling. Everything I knew said it was wrong to pressure him, but the voice inside kept insisting, *Pray for him now!*

I clasped my hand around his wrist in a halfhearted attempt to make him stand. Again, he shook his head sternly, like a fish trying to throw a hook. For some incomprehensible reason and by an invisible force, I began to pull him to his feet. No one was more surprised than I. Although I outweighed him by 50 pounds, he easily could have won a tug-of-war. At first, Tough Guy resisted, leaning and pulling in the opposite direction, but he was overpowered by the Spirit, arrested supernaturally, and taken into custody by the Holy Ghost.

The room fell silent as every eye in the place focused on Tough Guy. What would he do? Would the repressed anger buried just beneath his cool demeanor suddenly lash out, causing him to pull free? Would he take a swing at me? I watched him closely, but was calmly reassured that I was following orders.

He stood fully upright, still looking at the ground, but seemingly resigned to the fact that I was going to pray for him. I placed a hand on each side of his head and prayed quietly, alternating between tongues and English. After a few minutes, his forehead rested on my left shoulder, and he was perfectly still. The voice spoke softly, *Lay him down.*

You're kidding, I thought. *There is no way Tough Guy is going to be "slain in the Spirit." It is a miracle that he even let me pray for him!* Still, the voice softly said, *Lay him down.* Slowly, I removed my hands, but the young man did not seem to notice. *Lay him down!* the voice said firmly.

As I tried to tilt Tough Guy to one side, he slipped out of my grip. The dead weight of the stocky teenager was more than I could handle and he suddenly fell forward, dropping like a stone. A dozen people gasped at the same time. Tough Guy landed face down on the carpet, and I was sure he had injured himself, a broken nose at minimum. He did not respond to my question when I asked if he was okay. Instead, he lay perfectly still, frozen in position for 20 or 30 minutes.

In the days that followed, Tough Guy was still tough, but he changed also. He stopped avoiding eye contact and was able to receive from the Lord much more easily. He was almost always the last one to come for prayer, but he no longer resisted. He graduated from high school and stayed with Mark Rivera until he was 18, and since then has held a job in a nearby town.

Big Guy

A third young man caught my attention at the Anchor House that night. He was also a big guy. Although only 14 years old, he

78

was one of the tallest boys, big-boned and heavyset. It was the regular Thursday night chapel service and his first day at the house. Having been raised in a Lutheran home with no exposure at all to Pentecostal phenomena, "Big Guy" had never seen or heard of anyone falling under the power of God. During the prayer time, succumbing to the pressure of his peers, he stepped forward with his shoulders sloped, keeping his hands in his pockets. His speckled blue eyes peeked out from under his curly blond locks as if to ask, "What in the world is going on in this place?"

It was not so much that he was resistant, but absolutely clueless. Before I even had a chance to lift my hand to pray, the power of God blindsided him with a sucker punch that knocked all 175 pounds of Big Guy backward with such force that he took down several other boys with him. Everyone broke into spontaneous laughter at the sight of the completely uninitiated boy and his first encounter with the power of God. Big Guy could not possibly have faked it. For ten minutes he lay almost motionless exactly where he fell; only his eyelids flickered.

When Big Guy came around, he had no idea what had happened, but he knew that God was at the Anchor House. In the months that followed, he came for prayer on a regular basis, not asking for anything in particular, but simply experiencing the intimate presence of the Holy Spirit and growing steadily in his relationship with Jesus.

Most of our congregation were blessed by the revival, but the boys of Anchor House seemed to have received the most. They had many needs, and the Lord was pleased to minister to them personally, as well as through Mark Rivera and his staff.

Caught Unprepared

There was another group of people who were continually blessed by the revival at our church: visitors and newcomers. First-timers in any church are usually shy about participating. However, the revival brought a new breed of visitors who were forthcoming with their own needs and eager for prayer. They were like the magi who came to visit the baby Jesus, full of expectation and anticipation.

Most of the visitors came with the express purpose of being touched with the fresh anointing from the Lord. Often, they were hungrier than our regular members. At one point, in fact, it was not unusual to have more non-members come for prayer than old-timers. On the one hand, plenty of visitors was exactly what our congregation had always wanted; on the other hand, their presence presented a pastoral problem. Old members, especially those who were sitting on the fence about the revival, felt marginalized. They became spectators in their own congregation. "Who are all these strangers in our church?" remarked one woman. "I am starting to feel like a stranger myself."

The revival did reveal one awful thing; it exposed the attitudes of our hearts. The truth, it seemed, was that visitors were not really wanted or welcomed by everyone. It was much more comfortable to be a family church with the "right" kind of people who knew each other, than to acknowledge that we were only a small part of a much larger body, the Body of Christ. Still, I thought that the onslaught of visitors was good, if for no other reason than it put a burr under the saddle of the home folks and challenged them to keep seeking the Lord. The visitors also increased Sunday morning attendance by 50 percent.

Unfortunately, in the end, we did not incorporate many newcomers into our fellowship. Instead of adjusting to them, we expected newcomers to adapt to our rites and rituals. We were certain that if they stayed around long enough, they would learn to appreciate the liturgy. However, by not adjusting to the new make-up of the congregation—by not offering discipleship classes, for example—we did not retain many. Revival caught us off guard, and we did not adapt quickly enough.

Unpreparedness is a common problem that comes with revival. Rick Joyner described the effect of the Welsh Revival (1904-1905) on the church.

> "Almost every church or mission in the country grew dramatically, frequently doubling or even quadrupling in membership, and many maintained these members for years after the revival ended.

> "Even so, multitudes who were touched by the revival and had a genuine encounter with the Lord were also lost again to the world because there were not enough workers to care for them, to raise them spiritually."[3]

The Lakeland Revival came suddenly and unexpectedly, and we were caught flat-footed. It is doubtful that we could ever have fully prepared for revival even if we had known it was coming. Preparing for revival ahead of time would be almost like trying to learn how to swim from a book. Yet, if we had studied the history of revival before it came, we might have made more disciples.

The Old Who Would Not

Feeding the old sheep—the long-term members, whether young or old—was an even bigger challenge than feeding the newcomers. The former flock was used to a diet of mellow music, scriptural sermons, and the friendly style of a small church. Newcomers came to feast on the fresh spiritual food, but the nouvelle cuisine of revival did not appeal to some of the old-timers, and they let their discontent be known.

"Elvira" became a bleating sheep. She was "Miss Congeniality" of the parish, charming, full of stories and church anecdotes. Everyone made a fuss over her, and she enjoyed the attention; but as our numbers increased, she was lost in the crowd.

---

3.   Rick Joyner, *The World Aflame* (Charlotte, NC: Morning Star Publications, 1993), 77.

Miss Congeniality was comfortable with middle-of-the-road music and an attendance of 75 people on Sundays. Although she was a Christian and enjoyed seeing the young people get saved, she did not like contemporary music and felt overwhelmed when the number of regular worshipers doubled. It was too much for her. The newcomers distracted the attention that had once been paid to her, and the priority the congregation had once given to coffee and fellowship after the service was replaced with longer worship and a late lunch. At my suggestion, Elvira switched from the 10:00 a.m. service to the more intimate 8:00 a.m. service.

At first, it seemed like an agreeable solution, but soon there were cries of foul. The eight o'clockers happily welcomed Elvira to their quiet, hour-long Holy Communion. Miss Congeniality, however, missed her old friends and, "in confidence," complained to half of the people in the congregation.

"Mr. and Mrs. MacDonald" took me to task about Elvira. "You've made Miss Congeniality unhappy," they said. The Macs were charter members of the congregation and adopted grand-children of Elvira. They were friends and loved Elvira as much as I did, but the clock could not be turned back. Elvira muddled through, but the MacDonalds used the incident as an excuse to stop coming.

There were similar reactions from other mutton-headed sheep. They gave a variety of reasons for leaving the church, but their song was always the same: "Give me that old time religion, it's good enough for me." My decision to go full speed ahead with the revival left the disgruntled with four choices: switch to the traditional service, stay put with a scowl on their face, find new pasture, or jump into the revival river. Going back to the way things used to be was not an option.

One thing was clear—revival was not the end to pastoral problems. I remembered a sign that my father had posted on his boat: *Everyone Aboard Brings Joy: Some When They Come, Some When They Go.* Fran would not let me put the same sign in my office.

The Old Who Welcomed the New

Despite the negative attitude of some, God always sent encouragement from others. Gertrude had always been an encouragement to me, and she came through again when I needed her. One week, through the Sunday bulletin, I asked those who planned to leave the church to give us a chance to say good-bye. Gertrude, age 90, took my arm on her way out of church, "I hope you don't think I'm leaving." Gertrude said it was a joy to have a church where people were given a chance to receive Jesus just as she did when she was a teenager.

One Sunday morning there was a very loud message in tongues. I caught people glancing at Gertrude to see if she would flinch. Not a chance; she was like Anna in the temple, "looking forward to the redemption of Jerusalem."[4] When scores of people were "slain in the Spirit," Gertrude decided to give it a try. I really wanted to see God sweep her off her feet, but it did not happen. The second try had the same result, leaving her with the sad conclusion, "I guess it's not for me."

Of course, people experience God differently, but I did not agree with her conclusion. Despite her reluctance, I coaxed Gertrude to come forward a third time. When hands were laid upon her, she began to sway back and forth just a little. The Lord was touching her, but she was inhibited. It reminded me of a little child who needed a rest, but would not go to sleep. Finally, I asked if I could lay her gently back on the usher as I prayed for her. She agreed and finally relaxed and was lowered to the floor. She was willing, but needed a little help yielding. "That was wonderful," she said when she was back on her feet.

Deeper and Deeper

Revival fed the lambs, the hungry old sheep, and the shepherd as well. As the move of God penetrated deeper into my soul, I

---

4.   See Lk. 2:38b.

became more and more dependent on the Spirit. My devotions changed from telling God what I wanted to quietly sitting in the anointing. It was like floating on an inner tube, a simple prayer of oblation, an offering of myself.

Under the influence of the Spirit, I became unconscious of everything else. When I took time to sit in the presence of God, I felt the anointing being poured over me like oil. Sometimes it was like a mild current of electricity, gently vibrating my skin and causing my teeth to chatter as I became meek before the Lord. For the first few minutes, I fought to dismiss stray thoughts and worries. Gradually, I fell into a trance, not the kind associated with hypnotism or the occult, but a divine trance, the redirection of my thoughts from earthly to heavenly things. Like Martha's sister Mary, I "sat at the Lord's feet listening to what He said," having "chosen what is better, and it [would] not be taken away."[5]

The intimate times in God's presence were transforming. Sometimes He answered my questions about the revival; sometimes He built up my faith. Often, I did not want to come back to earth because it was much better to be caught up in the glory of God. Conversely, when I became too busy with temporal things and neglected the anointing time, my spiritual strength ran low, and I became irritable and anxious. When I returned to Him, His peace returned to me.

Everyone who hungered for a closer relationship with God was fed. Everyone who thirsted was satisfied. For everyone who was touched—young, old, pastor, parishioner, newcomer—it was like living in a dream, except that it was so very real. Revival brought us into a vital relationship with Jesus that challenged us at every point of our tradition, and for those who went with the flow, it filled and satisfied us in a way tradition never could.

---

5.   See Lk. 10:38-42.

Chapter Seven

Tradition and Revival

What does it take to convince people to change their habits and try something new? Why did Simon, Andrew, James, and John leave their family businesses to become fishers of men? What made Paul stop persecuting the Church and become the apostle to the Gentiles? How do you convince someone to break with the traditions of men and join in the new move of God?

With men it is impossible, but nothing is impossible with God. As a matter of fact, only an encounter with God can truly change people. In our experience of revival, we encountered three particular attitudes that pose resistance to change. First, many people who have been used to doing something the same way for 20 years interpret "change" as implying that there is something wrong with them. Never mind that the Bible says that all our righteousness is like filthy rags;[1] some people become defensive at the slightest hint that they are not living the perfect Christian life.

---

1.   See Is. 64:6.

Secondly, many people readily recognize the need for change in others without recognizing their own need for change. This is the old "mote-in-the-eye vs. beam-in-the-eye" syndrome.[2] On many occasions, groups who have been praying for revival have asked me to speak about the outbreak of revival in our congregation. They are usually enthusiastic about what happened until I say, "Revival must begin with you." Everyone wants God to revive their city; few want Him to begin on their own street.

The third reason people are resistant to change is that they simply see no need for it. Whether or not they are trapped in tradition, they are satisfied with the status quo; they are content with things as they are. They have no desire to change.

Released From Old Bonds

I remember one woman in particular who was resistant to the idea of revival. One Sunday I was the featured speaker at St. Bartholomew's Episcopal Church in Nashville, Tennessee. "Louise" arrived for the Sunday service in her dark green Jaguar, poised and self-assured. When I started praying for people, she remained glued to her seat, refusing to come forward. Her friend "Marianne" asked her, "Aren't you going up for prayer?"

"Absolutely not!" Louise replied firmly.

"Well, I'll pray for you to be open," Marianne responded.

Louise was indignant. "Don't you dare pray for me to be open! I'm perfectly satisfied with myself!"

Marianne hugged Louise and started praying anyway. The next thing Louise knew the two of them were standing in front of Father Montgomery (the pastor) and me. It went something like this: Louise said, "Okay, you guys, I'm not going to fall down, so don't push me. I'll just take the prayer, thank you."

---

2.   See Mt. 7:3-5 KJV.

Louise closed her eyes, tilted her head back, and prayed, "Father, forgive my sins. Take away my bonds." Her own words surprised her; "Take away my bonds" was not exactly in her every-day vocabulary.

"Receive," I commanded.

Louise prayed, "Lord, release me," and to her great surprise, she hit the floor!

While she was lying on the floor, her mouth moved involuntarily as she prayed in the Spirit. She could hear people talking, sort of like when the television is on while you're taking a nap—she could hear the voices, but focused only on what God was doing in her. In her mind she kept saying, "Lord, I don't know what You're doing, but whatever it is, don't let me up from this floor until You're finished!"

A few minutes later, Louise sat up to find Father Montgomery sitting beside her. She noticed her intense breathing and asked him, "Why am I breathing so deeply?" She took a few more deep breaths and then, *boom*, she was out again. The next time she came around, she felt light-headed and was still pondering what her deep breathing meant.

Set Free Into Peace

In the parish hall after the service, Louise asked Father Montgomery what he thought "the release" part meant. What was it all about? She didn't have a clue. He said, "I believe God released you from a past experience." He was referring to an experience she had confided to him at an earlier time. Later, in a letter to me, she described what had taken place.

"February 2, 1995

"Dear Father Williams,

I've been in the Episcopal Church for twenty-two years. I fell in love with the sacraments. I liked the liturgy. When hearing about your Holy Spirit revival, I was not happy about it at all. I complained to Father Montgomery, "If I wanted to go to a Pentecostal church, I'd go to the Assembly of God Church." I wanted St. Bartholomew's to stay just the same, thank you. After all, I had been there twenty years; Father Montgomery had been there only two. I've seen them come, and I've seen them go...this revival thing held no interest for me at all. I was perfectly happy with the status quo. Keep in mind, I was a "born-again, Spirit-filled (somewhat) believer." But, there was resistance! Real resistance! Deep down resistance! Rebellion!!! There was a blockage, and I didn't know why. Now I know.

He (Father Montgomery) was absolutely right, and as the next hours passed, I realized more and more the deliverance was from an incident that had traumatized my life for over thirty-four years! When I was seventeen years old, I was brutally gang-raped at knife point.

It was a trauma that would ultimately affect nearly every male relationship I ever had. I didn't know I was under a bondage from this experience. I had never thought about it in that way, even though I couldn't read a newspaper article about rape or watch a movie or television program about it. I would immediately turn the page or leave the room or switch the channel. I spent years counseling my daughter about being careful in parking lots, on campus, etc.

My story in a nutshell is this: Nearly every facet of my life was influenced by this one incident. My relationship with Jesus...I didn't know how to love Him. My relationship with the Father was a little easier because I had a wonderful earthly father, but still there was this resistance, resistance, resistance...a wall I didn't know was there...but it was there just the same.

Sunday morning I was delivered from the bondage of the distrust of men, of seeking men's approval...of rebellion. I don't understand it all...don't need to. I am still praying to "receive." I know now, that when I was released by God, the stress from that

34-year-old trauma held in my spirit was gone and I could breathe again like never before. Praise God! And, the funny feeling I couldn't figure out—the *peace of God*! I'm not sure I've ever been at peace.

If I close my eyes, I can still see "Mrs. Jaguar" with her well-coifed hair, designer eyeglasses, big silver earrings, and bold plaid jacket—absolutely perfect on the outside. Inside, in her heart, the place that Jesus cares about the most, she was bound by age-old wounds that prevented her from living the abundant life Jesus came to give. Although she had been born again and baptized with the Holy Spirit, God wanted to do more. He wanted to totally set her free, even though her own rebellious attitude resisted. Once she caught a glimpse of what the Lord was up to, once the grace of God matched her rebellion tit for tat, once she was touched again by her first love, she surrendered and received. In order for it to happen, she had to be willing to give up the comfortable and the familiar—the traditional.

Where's the Fire?

Sometimes God allows you to see a similar problem in someone else just to help you get the point. That is what happened to me when I saw the fruitlessness of the traditions of men reflected in the mirror of another church.

Three months after Palm Sunday, our congregation was burning hot with revival fire. Perhaps it was not the best time to leave for vacation, but my family was looking forward to our previously scheduled trip to New England. On the way north, we spent a few days in Washington, D.C., and on Sunday morning we walked down the street to attend one of the Capitol's historic churches.

The moment I stepped onto the curb and looked at the dignified, old building, nostalgia warmed my heart. Every detail was preserved with integrity: the large wooden doors, the gracefully arched windows, the bell tower. The entire building was a beautiful example of colonial architecture. Contemporary churches in central Florida usually look like stucco-coated shoe boxes—cost effective, but lacking beauty and grace. This old church was stately with character and tradition.

Inside the building were more sensory delights: old, dark pews coated with a patina that only comes with age, air that was a little musty and scented with honey from the beeswax candles, shafts of light that filtered through stained-glass windows and reflected off the polished brass lectern. It reminded me of my early days in the Episcopal church at St. Mary's, Madison, and Holy Comforter in Tallahassee, where Fran and I were married. The emotional lure of tradition and fond memories tugged at my heart.

The service in the old church was a mixture of biblical, liturgical, and historical traditions. It began with the processional of ministers and choir, marching in by rank in vestments of freshly pressed white cottas over cassocks of blue and red. The senior minister was clad in a traditional white robe, gathered at his waist with a long rope and a silk damask stole around his neck.

I couldn't help chuckling a little as I thought about the contrast between a revival church and the venerable old museum in which we sat. Thousands attended the Lakeland Revival, but here the congregation was sparse, even for a summer morning—only about 50, including our family of four. Revival services were loud and rollicking; here the old church was silent, formal, and still.

Our son, Hugh, age ten and the fisherman in the family, stared down at the floor as if watching his cork for signs of a bite. Our daughter, Elizabeth, age 13, the dancer and diplomat, smiled with amusement when her glance and thoughts connected with mine. Fran, the "cradle Episcopalian" with bishops in her family line, enduringly rolled her eyes toward the ceiling. We felt uncomfortable and out of place, gasping for air and trying to find a note of inspiration in the beautiful but desperately boring service.

We were used to meetings that lasted four hours, and although we knew we would be out much sooner, each minute in the "Washington archives" seemed like an eternity. The preacher, an interim pastor, preached a tolerably good sermon. A quartet of paid professionals sang the anthem a cappella in four-part harmony. Including communion, the service was over in less than an hour.

Why was it so tedious? On the surface everything was spit and polished: the architecture, the atmosphere, the liturgy, and the music. Hollywood could have filmed a movie on the first take. It was like a wax museum, the perfect tableau of 18th-century American religion. All the forms were there; the images were complete. The only thing missing was any discernible presence of the Lord. There was a form of godliness—an attempt at full spirituality—but there was no power.[3] A twinkle of gospel light glimmered in the sermon, but there was no joy, no invitation to receive Jesus, no laying on of hands, no testimony about mended hearts, captives set free, or changed lives.

Some questions stirred inside me throughout the service. Could what happened in Lakeland happen anywhere? Sure, our church had been like a wax museum and revival had come, but at least ours was a charismatic fellowship to start with. Does God want to revive every church, or are some sunk so deep in tradition that they cannot be raised? *Could revival kindle a fire even in this wax museum?*

Stuck in the Mud

The apostle Paul spoke of two kinds of tradition. There is godly tradition:

Therefore, brethren, stand fast, and hold the traditions which ye have been taught, whether by word, or our epistle (2 Thessalonians 2:15 KJV).

---

3.   See 2 Tim. 3:5.

There are the traditions of men:

I was advancing in Judaism beyond many Jews of my own age and was extremely zealous for the traditions of my fathers (Galatians 1:14).

Jesus charged the Pharisees[4] with hypocrisy for letting go of *the commandments of God* and holding to *the traditions of men.*[5] The sin was not tradition itself, but substituting tradition for the commands of God. Neither should we be rooted so deeply in tradition that we are unable to follow the move of the Holy Spirit today.

One morning I was sitting next to Sister Alice at a retreat for 57 Roman Catholic priests. During a moment of silence at the morning Eucharist, she began to speak. It sounded like a prophecy, but I had never heard anything like it.

"Mud! Mud! Mud! Mud! You're all stuck in the mud! Get out of the mud. God says, 'Get out of the mud!' He does not want you to be stuck in the mud."

She might just as well have said, "Tradition! Tradition! Tradition! God does not want you stuck in tradition." Or, "Rut! Rut! Rut! God does not want you to be stuck in a rut!" Mud and ruts are metaphors for tradition. All of these represent hindrances that keep us from following the Spirit of God.

Something Old, Something New

Tradition is not limited to traditional churches. After my own experience of revival, an Assembly of God church invited me to speak at their Sunday evening meeting. Before the service began, the pastor, who had also been touched at the Lakeland Revival,

---

4. For further information on the resistance to the Holy Spirit and Pharisaism, see William DeArteaga, *Quenching the Spirit* (Lake Mary, FL: Creation House, 1992, 1996).
5. See Mk. 7:8.

took me into his office, "I want to prepare you for the fact that few people in this congregation have seen signs and wonders."

That surprised me. I was looking forward to ministering in a congregation who valued the move of the Holy Ghost. When I asked him why, his answer described not only his own congregation, but Pentecostals in general. "The people at this service are third-generation Pentecostals. Their *grandparents* experienced the move of the Spirit, but they have only heard about it."

That night, the service began exactly like the Baptist church down the street: an opening hymn, a call to worship, special choir music, a pastoral prayer, the offering followed by a solo, and a puppet show for the children. We sang a few contemporary praise choruses, but the worship was not anointed nor was the Spirit manifested. There were no tongues or prophecy. It was a Pentecostal wax museum.

One hundred fifty people were sprinkled throughout the fifteen-hundred seat auditorium, mostly toward the back. They were not forthcoming with reactions to my message, so I took the ministry to them. I called people from their seats in much the same way that I had seen it done at the Lakeland Revival. The first two people did not respond, but by the end of the meeting, almost everyone had come forward to receive a touch from the Spirit of God. One rather large woman who was shrieking and laughing had to be carried from the building by the ushers. Something new had overcome something old. Revival fire began to melt the traditions of men.

Confronting Tradition

Someone else who was completely overcome by the new move of God was my wife, Fran. Since she was from a long-standing Episcopalian family, members of our congregation often looked to her as a bellwether of what was within the bounds of Anglican acceptability. Parishioners who were afraid to approach me turned to her with the question: "What do you think of the revival?" Fran's reaction was straightforward.

"I feel like a backyard dog that has been let out the front door!" She meant no disrespect to her upbringing, only that there was a wonderful new freedom that came with revival. Fran grew up reciting an Anglican liturgy that was heavily penitential. For example, during the Communion service the priest said the Prayer of Humble Access: "We are not worthy so much as to gather up the crumbs under Thy table, O, Lord...." Fran received Jesus in 1969 and ten years later received the baptism of the Holy Spirit and the gift of tongues. The revival, however, was the time when her emotions connected with the Church's teaching and tradition. No longer did she merely say "Hallelujah"; she shouted *"Hallelujah!"*

Revival forced much of our "church family tradition" to take a back seat to what we saw God doing today. Changing the lives of living saints became priority number one. The Holy Ghost was making new tracks. Revival began with a desire to change, not a desire to rebel or to abandon tradition. We simply wanted to follow Jesus more closely.

The Palm Sunday watershed brought us face-to-face with God, and face-to-face with the fruitlessness of many of our traditions. Revival focused our eyes clearly on Jesus. He became the issue, the program, and the purpose of the parish. The new move of God collided with some of our most cherished traditions, most notably the time limit. However, with Jesus leading the charge, church school problems were solved, financial struggles disappeared, and an enormous weight was lifted off both the congregation and the pastor.

The revival was wonderful, and our congregation as a whole was blessed tremendously and brought closer to the Lord. Even during revival, however, there was not always calm waters and smooth sailing. There was conflict and criticism, sometimes harsh. When the conflict of change became particularly intense, we were sometimes tempted to abandon the revival and "return to Egypt." People we loved left the church stamping their sandals in the dust with the curse that we were no longer Episcopalians. That accusation really hurt, but one thing that kept us going was the abundant fruit that revival produced in us. That fruit had room to grow once the smothering vines of tradition were pruned away. Amidst the joy of the "new wine" and the unsettledness of adjusting to the "new way," we discovered the sobering truth that not only does revival bring blessings, it also carries costs.

Chapter Eight

The Cost of Revival

Heaven-sent revival was pouring down like rain, but not everyone wanted to get wet. Some, whose faith was dry, preferred to stay that way, even some who proudly called themselves charismatics. In fact, some "Spirit-filled" folks were among the first to reject what most saw as a sovereign move of God. It gave us an eery insight into what Jesus must have experienced when the very people He came to save rejected Him. Every pastor grieves a bit when he loses sheep, even sheep on the fringe of the flock. During revival, the flock was culled weekly, forcing us continually to make a choice: Let go of the sheep, or let go of God.

Uneasy Evangelists

Can we have the new without giving up the old? Apparently not. The first price we paid was a decrease in membership; about 20 percent of the congregation left within the first year after the revival came. Most of those who left, we never saw again. Sunday morning attendance increased, but not without a major shake-up.

Some old and faithful members switched to the quieter eight o'clock service, while others stopped coming all together. It raised a tough question: If the Spirit of God had come to revive the Body of Christ, why were people bailing out? There were plenty of excuses.

Just when evangelism was becoming effortless, the couple in charge of our evangelism program, "Mr. and Mrs. E," resigned and left the church. A retired couple, the "E's" were away visiting their family when the revival hit. Upon their return, the former smiling front-row sitters looked glum. Almost everyone else was happy, particularly the steady stream of teenagers who responded to the altar call each week to be saved. Yet Mr. and Mrs. E looked more distressed each Sunday.

Weeks before it happened, I knew that the E's would leave the church. Each succeeding Sunday, they sat closer to the back. When they reached the last row and could retreat no further, they spoke to me.

"God has called us to a new ministry," began Mrs. E, the more talkative of the two.

"Really?" I said, trying to act surprised.

"Mr. E and I have prayed about it, and we wanted to tell you that we will not be attending church here anymore. God is calling us to move on."

This scenario occurred often enough for me to have a pat answer. My usual reply was, "Thank you for your service. We will miss you. God bless you. You know you are always welcome here. Don't forget to write." This time, however, I decided to forego the usual pleasantries and ask the obvious question. "Where has God called you?"

"Oh, we don't know that," said Mrs. E with perfect sincerity. "We just believe that He is leading us somewhere else."

I would rather she had said something like, "You are ugly; your wife is a shrew; your children are brats; the church is too cold; we hate the music"; or whatever the real reason was. Why couldn't she simply tell the truth? Did she even know it? Or was it that they were ill at ease because the Holy Spirit now spontaneously inspired evangelism? Could it be that they were unhappy and felt out of place because what was once considered "their" ministry was now unnecessary?

Dearly Departed Disciples

It has been said that an *excuse* is the skin of a reason stuffed with a lie. The excuse most people gave for leaving the church usually developed like the story of "Mr. and Mrs. T." Formerly, they were smiling charismatics, but they turned to ice and stone. While jubilation, joy, and laughter filled everyone around them, the T's sat motionless with their eyes closed or looking at the floor. I could have filled out the transfer papers on the spot. Within a week or two, the T's stopped attending, so I gave them a call to ask if everything was all right.

"Yes, of course, everything is fine. We have been so busy lately, and Little T has had a bad cold. We love you and Fran and everyone in the congregation, but we decided we needed a change." In true Episcopalian fashion, they had voted with their feet. Rather than say anything to anyone, they had silently tiptoed out the back door.

For others, the newly kindled light of Christ was too bright; it exposed the sin in their lives. One active member of the congregation said to me, "My wife and I aren't comfortable here anymore." Years later I discovered why; he had been having an adulterous affair. Revival revealed hidden sin in the church. Some folks repented and enjoyed a new relationship with Jesus, while others headed for the hills.

"Robin" boasted about being a long-time charismatic and was outspoken in his disapproval of the revival. Instead of leaving, however, he decided to stay and make trouble. It wasn't long before we found out why he criticized the revival. Although not a member of our congregation, he complained to our bishop that I was ruining the finances of the church. Being accused of financial mismanagement motivated me to do something I had resisted during 18 years of ministry: I asked the parish secretary to pull Robin's giving record. "I don't have to," she said. "He gives the same thing every week—five dollars."

Robin retired early and settled in Florida with two new cars and a four-bedroom home with a swimming pool. Apparently, he liked church much better when he could have his cake and eat it too. When the fire of God heated up his wallet, he became uncomfortable. The fire came to refine, and refining meant change—a change that he resisted.

Holy Distractions

Every congregation loses peripheral members, and persuading stray sheep to return to the flock is almost impossible. However, when the core members become restless, it is a more serious matter. "Bill" was the Senior Warden (the ranking layman of the church) a cattleman, and a very practical gentleman. His church background was Baptist, but his wife, "Julie," was a former Roman Catholic. Bill and Julie were our friends, and they did a lot to help the church, including hosting an annual church picnic at their ranch. One day Bill phoned to express his concern about the laughter during Holy Communion. "What do you think about what is going on at Communion? We're all for the revival, but a couple of people told me they aren't too sure about it. The laughter at Communion bothers them because the sacrament is supposed to be holy. I just thought you ought to know."

All the questions and doubts I had already worked through came to the front of my mind again as I brooded over the phone call. My discernment meter was still pegged all the way to the right about the revival—"It's God...it's God...it's God"—but criticism from the leadership made me worry. My wife Fran is a prophetess

100

with a sense of humor, and she said to me, "Why pray when you can worry? It is so much easier to worry because worry requires no faith." After agonizing for some time over Bill's phone call, I prayed.

"Lord, these people You gave me are a little upset. They say that the laughter on Sunday morning is distracting. Some say they cannot hear the Bible readings and the sermon because of all the noise. I know *holy* does not mean 'silent,' but the laughter during Communion is upsetting people. They say the signs and wonders are distracting. Now Lord, I am the one who has to listen to these bleating sheep, and I think even You will admit they have a point."

That inner voice spoke to me. *Yes, it **is** distracting, but it is **I** who am distracting you. I am taking your mind off of what **you** have been doing and putting it on what **I** am doing **now**!*

Silence and holy awe fell on me as I meditated on what the Lord said. God, it seemed, wanted to draw our attention away in another direction, but some perceived His leadership as a distraction from the way we had always done things. If the church was to be revived, it meant dying to the old and yielding to the new work of the Spirit. It meant doing exactly what Jesus did—paying a price.

Someone has humorously defined *insanity* as "doing the same thing over and over again, but expecting different results." That was an apt description of our attitude. Subconsciously we did the same thing year after year expecting that one day God would bless us with prosperity and growth. The truth, which was now becoming evident, was that we would have to change. Death was a prerequisite for resurrection.

Controversy

Revivals are characterized by revitalization, conversions, and controversy. When the 19th-century revivalist Charles Finney gave the first modern-styled altar call, there was a storm of criticism. In those days, Presbyterian parishioners were taught that people could do nothing about their own salvation; if they were one of the elect, the Holy Spirit would convert them. Finney's demand for an immediate free will decision caused such anger that it was reported that he was going to be tarred and feathered.[1] Today, however, Charles Finney is among the most revered figures in revival history.

In classic revival tradition, we were plunged into a fountain of glory and a storm of criticism. More than once, fellow priests and parishioners tarred us with the brush of being too Pentecostal, in need of therapy, or trying to emulate the Assemblies of God. When revival came, we welcomed the conversions and the joy, but the condemnation surprised us. Pastors like to think they are doing a good job when all is calm in the fold. They do not like restless sheep. One reason revivals do not last is that leaders want conversion without conflict. However, conflict is unavoidable because revival amplifies the clash between two kingdoms—the Kingdom of Heaven and the kingdom of this world.

Think about it. When did Jesus ever show up without causing controversy? The mere report of his birth so threatened King Herod that he had the young boys of Bethlehem slaughtered, and His years of ministry were certainly not peaceful and predictable.[2] "Jesus put His fingers into the man's ears. Then He spit and touched the man's tongue."[3] He spit on another man eyes.[4] He made saliva mud and put it on yet another man's eyes.[5] Jesus cast demons into pigs, "and the whole herd rushed down the steep bank into the lake and died in the water."[6] "He made a whip out of cords, and drove all from the temple area, both sheep and cattle;

---

1. *America's Great Revivals* (Minneapolis: Bethany House Publishers), 73.
2. "When Herod realized that he had been outwitted by the Magi, he was furious, and he gave orders to kill all the boys in Bethlehem and its vicinity who were two years old and under..." (Mt. 2:16).
3. Mk. 7:33b.
4. See Mk. 8:23.
5. See Jn. 9:1-7
6. Mt. 8:32b.

He scattered the coins of the money changers and overturned their tables."[7] In the end He died a criminal's death, bloody, bruised, and beaten.

Revival brought revolution. Remember the words of Paul: "Yea, and all that will live godly in Christ Jesus shall suffer persecution."[8] Finally, our church had conversions, but what an uproar! Bitter hostility came with the sweet fruit. We were not tarred and feathered, but the deafening screams from those who opposed the fresh anointing of Jesus almost shouted us down.

The loss of both members and the support of leaders was the most difficult thing to accept. As pastor, I was torn between rejoicing in what I knew was an extraordinary move of God and watching people I cared for draw back from the church. It was painfully frustrating to see people turn away from what the Lord was doing. I began to understand what was in Jesus' heart when He turned over the tables of the money changers and mourned over Jerusalem.

> O Jerusalem, Jerusalem, you who kill the prophets and stone those sent to you, how often I have longed to gather your children together, as a hen gathers her chicks under her wings, but you were not willing. Look, your house is left to you desolate. For I tell you, you will not see Me again until you say, "Blessed is He who comes in the name of the Lord" (Matthew 23:37-39).

I did not dare to say it openly, but I began to wonder if we were experiencing something even more radical than revival, perhaps a complete reformation of the Church. Was Christ ushering in changes in the Church that were far greater and deeper than at any other time in history?

---

7.   Jn. 2:15.
8.   2 Tim. 3:12 KJV.

Shaking Us Out of Our Comfort Zone

...unless you change and become like little children, you will never enter the kingdom of heaven (Matthew 18:3).

Changes in the church were radical and rapid, and were naturally met with suspicion by many. Something we had always dreamed of became reality. *"Suddenly"* we were in the book of Acts:[9]

*They were looking intently up into the sky as He was going, when **suddenly** two men dressed in white stood beside them* (Acts 1:10).

***Suddenly** a sound like the blowing of a violent wind came from heaven and filled the whole house where they were sitting* (Acts 2:2).

Revival brought sudden change, and sudden change provoked funny reactions from people: Pretend like nothing had happened; try to control it; act as though this is nothing new to us; try not to offend anyone. The pastor of a large South African church that was reluctant to flow with revival expressed a common fear: "We have worked hard to build up our church, and we don't want to lose people." While this is a perfectly understandable attitude, it is important to remember that revival is God's attempt to clean up and restore the Church to the way *He* wants it, not to give the Good Housekeeping seal of approval to the way we are doing things at present. For our congregation, that meant yielding and giving up control. We had to allow the Lord to shake things up, even though it pushed us out of our comfort zone.

If those who ignored earthly warnings didn't get away with it, what will happen to us if we turn our backs on heavenly warnings? His voice that time shook the earth to its foundations; this time–He's told us this quite plainly–He'll also rock the heavens:

---

9. Other "suddenly" Scriptures in the Book of Acts include: 8:39; 9:3-4; 10:30; 12:6-7; 12:10; 16:25-26.

The Cost of Revival

"One last shaking, from top to bottom, stem to stern." The phrase "one last shaking" means a thorough house-cleaning, getting rid of all the historical and religious junk so that the essentials stand clear and uncluttered. Do you see what we've got? An unshakeable kingdom! And do you see how thankful we must be? Not only thankful, but brimming with worship, deeply reverent before God. For God is not an indifferent bystander. He's actively cleaning house, torching all that needs to burn, and He won't quit until it's all cleansed. God Himself is Fire! (Hebrews 12:25-29 The Message)

The Lord is a shaker; He shakes churches and He shakes pastors. I gladly would have signed on as the administrator of revival, but there was no such job opening. The first course in the school of revival leadership is not theory but a personal trip through the fiery furnace of change. I had to face up to some very personal questions. Was I willing to pay the price of revival, to let the Lord change me as much as He was changing the people in the congregation? Promoting sudden and radical change in a traditional denomination like mine could mean losing my job. Was I willing to sacrifice my congregation, my salary, my pension, and even my ordination if necessary? All too glibly I answered "yes," not realizing that the Lord would one day accept the sacrifice. I had no idea of the changes that lay ahead.

More Than We Bargained For

The revival brought signs, wonders, miracles, and dramatic change. Mr. Lee Buck, an evangelist and a former executive vice president of New York Life Insurance Company, once told me that making too many changes too often is one of the seven deadly sins of management. That is good advice, generally speaking, but what if God is the One making the changes?

Then there was the problem of those who did not want to change. Many folks said by their words or their actions, "I'm okay where I am." This kind of an attitude is very frustrating for a pastor. How do you lead people who do not want to go anywhere? Others said, "We like the church the way it used to be." Great! Now we even had some who wanted to proceed *backwards*! I began to experience the same frustration Jesus must have felt when He tried to lead His disciples.

> *Aware that His disciples were grumbling about this, Jesus said to them, "Does this offend you? What if you see the Son of Man ascend to where He was before! The Spirit gives life; the flesh counts for nothing. The words I have spoken to you are spirit and they are life. Yet there are some of you who do not believe." For Jesus had known from the beginning which of them did not believe and who would betray Him. He went on to say, "This is why I told you that no one can come to Me unless the Father has enabled him." From this time many of His disciples turned back and no longer followed Him* (John 6:61-66).

At times, I was tempted to have a reverse altar call: "This morning I would like to see the hands of everyone whose life is a perfect reflection of the glory of God; every step you take is on the path of righteousness, every word you speak is anointed; you are completely filled with the Holy Spirit and do not need to change a thing. Now, I want those of you who raised your hands to stand to your feet. Right now, step into the aisle, turn to the back of the church and walk out the door. Ushers are waiting to see you to your cars."

Another pastor in North Carolina in whose church I ministered one Sunday felt a similar frustration. When only a few of the 400-member congregation responded to my invitation to come forward for prayer, this brother gave his folks a piece of his mind:

> "I cannot believe what I am seeing. I am your pastor and I know you. I know there are lots of you with needs in your lives, needs that only the Lord can meet. The Spirit of God is moving up here, but you are just sitting comfortably in your seats. Okay! If that's the way you want it,

just sit there. But don't call me on the phone Monday morning and say, 'Pastor, I need to come in and talk to you about a problem.' "

A Vision of Heaven

In spite of the grumbling, I still believed that God was at work in our church in a mighty way, and I wanted more than ever to be in the middle of it. My faith was stronger than it had ever been; my zeal was like pure Holy Ghost adrenaline. No longer did I simply step into a room. Everywhere I went, I burst through the door expecting the Lord to perform a miracle. My attitude was, "Let's stop quibbling about words and get on with what Jesus wants to do!" With the fresh anointing I knew how Jeremiah felt with "a fire shut up in [his] bones."[10]

After my personal revival at Carpenter's Home Church, I attended every revival meeting for the next six weeks before a previous commitment drew me away. The annual Clergy and Spouse Conference was one of my favorite getaways; Fran and I had missed it only once in the 13 years we had been in the Diocese of Central Florida. In 1993, I felt torn away from the revival meetings, but I discovered that the anointing traveled with me. Overflowing joy bubbled in my soul. Tremendous excitement about the cosmic-scale revival rumbled like thunder in my heart.

The conference opened with singing, and as I joined in wholeheartedly, I was overcome by the Spirit and sank slowly to the floor. I knew it would raise a few eyebrows from some of my fellow priests, but I decided to yield to the impulse of God no matter where I was.

Those clergy at the conference who were baptized in the Holy Spirit were eager to hear about our experience. Karen Howe, our

---

10.   "But if I say, 'I will not mention Him or speak any more in His name,' His word is in my heart like a fire, a fire shut up in my bones. I am weary of holding it in; indeed, I cannot" (Jer. 20:9).

bishop's wife, was especially excited, and I hoped the bishop would be too. During the social hour on the second night of the conference, I told the bishop about the meetings and urged him to attend. His response surprised me. "If God can do something about that man over there, I'd be interested." (Bishop Howe told me later that he was not challenging God but trying to stir up my faith.)

He pointed to an elderly man who had a large white bandage covering the right side of his face. Deacon Dee Erdman had cancer, and doctors had removed his voice box. He spoke using a small handheld vibrator that he pressed against his throat. As I watched him sitting with his wife, Letty, on the sofa I prayed, "Lord, do You want to do something about Dee?" The Lord's reply was immediate and abrupt. *Yes!*

Bishop Howe gave me permission to pray for the deacon at the evening program as long as I had Dee's permission in advance. Both Dee and Letty were eager for prayer. Before the evening program, I announced to the clergy and their spouses that we had a brother who desired prayer and that the bishop had given permission to pray for him following the meeting.

That night, I could not concentrate on the lecture. I sat restlessly as the Spirit prepared me for ministry. When the program concluded, I asked Dee and Letty to join me on the platform. I sensed the Lord was about to move in a powerful way, but to my own surprise, I did not pray for healing. Instead, I found myself asking God to glorify Himself in Dee Erdman. Dee began to tremble, gently at first, then stronger. He looked up and appeared to notice something on the ceiling.

"Do you see something?" I asked. Dee nodded. "Are you seeing a vision?" He nodded again. "Is it a vision of Heaven?" Again, Dee nodded slowly and was trembling. He watched for awhile longer as tears streamed down his cheeks. Then he lifted his hands and mouthed with his lips the words, "Praise the name of Jesus!"

After a few more minutes, he pressed the vibrator to his throat, and turning to his wife, said, "Angels. I see angels!"

Message From the Enemy

We ended in silence. Unnoticed by me was the fact that one-third of the clergy had already left. Many of them were offended by my prayer ministry and wrote letters to the bishop telling him so. One of them, an old, liberal windbag, confronted me the next morning at the breakfast buffet. "I have a word for you," he puffed. "Last night, I was awakened by an angel at 2:00 a.m. He gave me a message and said that I must give it to you."

A cold, sullen, tingling sensation gripped my legs from the knees down. Something did not ring true. I was surprised that "Old Windbag" even spoke to me, but even more surprised that an angel had spoken to him.

"Yes?" I replied skeptically.

His face turned ashen and his lips quivered as he said, "The angel said to tell you that your soul is in mortal danger. Your parish is in great peril, and you must repent immediately and seek help."

The chill at my knees moved up my legs, freezing my whole body. Paralyzing fear came over me, and I felt nauseated. This message was from the accuser, and his flaming dart had found its mark. It hurt, not so much in the sense that I was offended, but that a man who called himself a priest of the church would yield to such evil words. I turned away and walked quickly in the opposite direction.

Anointed for Death

Six weeks later, I heard that Dee Erdman had gone to be with the Lord. I was terribly disappointed because I had assumed that he would be healed. When I phoned his wife, she described what happened following the clergy-spouse conference. "After that evening, Dee had a fabulous month of strength before he died.

The funeral was magnificent, full of music and joy. Dee's brother was dumbfounded. He hated funerals, but said he had never seen such love in a church. Once, when I looked at him out of the corner of my eye, I think I saw him raising his hands."

Months later, I began to understand what had happened. Dee was anointed before he died just like Jesus was anointed before His death. Dee died with a vision of Heaven. Jesus said,

> *Let not your heart be troubled: ye believe in God, believe also in Me. In My Father's house are many mansions: if it were not so, I would have told you. I go to prepare a place for you. And if I go and prepare a place for you, I will come again, and receive you unto myself; that where I am, there ye may be also* (John 14:1-3 KJV).

A few weeks later, I visited my aunt and uncle in Texas who were Methodists and knew very little about the Pentecostal experience. Charismatic protocol calls for "cooling it" around denominational Christians. It is best to avoid arguments and their wrathful prejudice against "Holy Rollers." I planned to avoid confrontation and keep quiet about the revival. If the subject of religion came up, I would hasten to say, "Tell me about your church." The only problem was the fire shut up in my bones. It was impossible to be quiet. When my aunt asked how my church was going, I told her.

"We're having revival," I said, swallowing hard. "Almost everyone we pray for falls under the power. When we pray for them, they fall backward and lie on the floor for extended periods of time."

Without missing a beat, my aunt said, "Well, then you're a witch."

Grace caught up with me, and I let the conversation drop. My aunt did not really believe I was a witch. She simply reacted the way many people do, by relegating all spiritual things they do not understand to the realm of evil spirits and the occult. I let it pass. Misunderstanding change is a part of revival.

We Have Been Waiting for This!

Criticism, no matter what the issue, usually focused on me personally. If criticism is the price of leadership, this move of God came with a very expensive price tag. Christians who are used to boarding a ship sitting in dry dock become seasick when it is launched. Misinformed, they think the pastor is the captain of the church and blame him or her for everything that happens. The truth is that God is the captain. He sends the rising water of revival to launch the ship because He wants to go fishing.

In the middle of a flood of changes and its accompanying criticism, my wife, Fran, was the greatest comfort to me. She helped me to put things into perspective and to get over the hurtful remarks people made about me. Once, when someone asked if she was "in favor of the revival," she commented, "Are you kidding? We've been waiting for this!" Those words summed up my feelings too. They gave me courage to persevere, even through a firestorm of unfavorable reactions.

Nevertheless, the majority of our congregation was hungry for God. They worked hard during the week calling on the sick, following up on visitors, and maintaining the church grounds. On Sunday, they worshiped and enjoyed themselves, basking in the glory of the Lord. They were changing, becoming more like Jesus, even amidst persecution and criticism. The cost of revival was high, but the rewards infinitely outweighed the cost.

Chapter Nine

Called on the Carpet

...*"The harvest is plentiful, but the workers are few. Ask the Lord of the harvest, therefore, to send out workers..."* (Luke 10:2).

Revival came with incredible power. Like a bolt of lightning that strikes a tree and runs along the ground, it hit our parish and immediately radiated out in all directions. It cut through our congregation like a sword and divided us into three camps. The largest was the 50 percent who sat on the fence with a wait-and-see attitude about the revival. Next was the 30 percent who were drawn to the revival and felt compelled to run with the fire. The final 20 percent were those who ran *from* the fire.

I found myself divided as well. My first calling was as the pastor of Christ the King Episcopal Church. Very soon, however, I received a new calling to a ministry I had never desired—itinerant evangelist. I don't remember the exact date. During the Lakeland Revival meetings, days and nights flowed together as our spirits seemed to travel in an orbit that reached from earth to Heaven. I remember only that the call came in the springtime of 1993.

During that particular meeting, Brother Rodney suddenly stopped in mid-sentence. There was a sudden shift in the service as if the wind of the Spirit had changed course and was now blowing from a different direction. The evangelist said, "I want to pray for all the pastors." That in itself was not unusual. Brother Rodney prayed for the ministers almost every night. I tried to take advantage of every opportunity to have another drink of the "new wine." So, in eager anticipation, I jogged onto the platform.

Three hundred pastors and their spouses came for prayer that night. Standing close to them in the prayer line, I could see exhaustion, hurt, rejection, disappointment, and despair etched into their faces. Tears traced their way along crow's-feet, as eyes turned upward toward Heaven. Standing there shoulder to shoulder, we were starved for divine affection. It was not easy trying to focus on Jesus in the midst of so many distractions—ushers scampering about, people falling, and the noise of laughter. Apparently, concentration was not essential. The anointing poured over everyone with the same result: Pastor after pastor fell on the vast platform of Carpenter's Home Church.

"Fill. Fill. Fill." The evangelist and self-styled "Holy Ghost Bartender" dispensed the "new wine."[1] When he came to me, I suddenly but gently fell facedown on the rose-colored carpet. The posture was unusual, but not uncomfortable. At first, nothing much seemed to happen; I did not feel anything. *Lord, do You want to tell me something?*

---

1. "Others mocking said, These men are full of new wine. But Peter, standing up with the eleven, lifted up his voice, and said unto them, Ye men of Judaea, and all ye that dwell at Jerusalem, be this known unto you, and hearken to my words: for these are not drunken, as ye suppose, seeing it is *but* the third hour of the day. But this is that which was spoken by the prophet Joel; and it shall come to pass in the last days, saith God, I will pour out of My Spirit upon all flesh..." (Acts 2:13-17 KJV).

The inner voice spoke to my spirit. *I am making you an evangelist.*

For all that the word *evangelist* meant to me, God might as well have said, "I'm making you an astronaut"; it would have had the same effect. I did not want to be an evangelist, and there were no evangelists I greatly admired. Even the ones I invited to our congregation often brought more problems than solutions. Nevertheless, I decided to file away the notion on the outside chance that it might be some sort of prophecy to be fulfilled in the distant future.

God's message to me was simple and clear: *Go where I tell you to go, pray what I tell you to pray, and say what I tell you to say, but no more.* The implication, however, was obscure. I did not ponder what it meant; if it happened, it happened.

Holy Ghost Classroom

It happened. As I regained my equilibrium, stood up, and began to walk back to my pew, a young man approached me. "Excuse me. I am from the Church on the Way in Palmetto, Florida. My pastor asked me to invite you to minister at our Friday night camp meeting."

That was quick, I thought. Forty-five seconds after being made an evangelist, and I already had my first invitation. *An invitation to where? Palmetto, Florida? Where on earth is that? I did not have a clue. The Church on the Way? On the way to where? Camp meeting? Does that mean you bring your own tent and lantern?*

That same week I received four other invitations to preach. Occasionally, a parish priest like myself is invited to substitute at a neighboring church or to speak at a Lenten lecture series. However, in 16 years of ministry, I had never received five invitations in one week, and rarely an invitation to minister outside the Episcopal church.

God directs the affairs of His people; the Bible makes that clear. Sensing the hand of God moving me around like a pawn on a chess board was an overwhelming and humbling experience. It was blessing enough to be spiritually refreshed by the revival and to have fire from Heaven melt away the wax-coated traditions in my mind. Yet, to hear the voice of God and see His arm open doors before me was astounding.

A great adventure commenced. Each new day raised the question, "What is God going to do next?" Personal concerns, goals, and ambitions evaporated like a morning mist. The Lord, it seemed, had launched a cosmic construction project and had hired me on as a laborer. As I mentioned before, one of the most notable changes was in the altar call. Prior to the beginning of my new ministry, altar calls had been extremely awkward with few responses. The fresh anointing changed that overnight, although for awhile my invitations continued to be clumsy. People responded anyway. It was not my finesse or strategy that drew them, but the Spirit of God.

My new calling was coupled with a new unction. When Samuel anointed David to replace Saul as king, David received both the purpose and the power to do the job. My experience was the same—the call to evangelism included the muscle to accomplish the mission. The anointing contained the power of God to accomplish the purpose of God. The "purpose and power" lesson was a personal revelation to me and a paradigm for revival. God refreshed the anointing on His people not simply to brighten up the Church, but to equip His people to do His work. Fresh anointing revived God's purpose and brought new power to the Church to carry out Christ's commission to make disciples of all nations.[2]

Fortunately, the fresh anointing also came with a built-in teacher. Seminary had given me a theological education, but no instruction on how to be an evangelist. The Spirit imparted the power and wisdom to accomplish God's purpose—sort of an on-line technical support. Unprepared, inexperienced, and unknowledgeable

2.   See Mt. 28:18-20.

about evangelism, I had no time to take a course and few models to follow. However, a passage in John's first epistle opened my eyes:

As for you, the anointing you received from Him remains in you, and you do not need anyone to teach you. But as His anointing teaches you about all things and as that anointing is real, not counterfeit–just as it has taught you, remain in Him (1 John 2:27).

The key was to "remain in Him." On paper that was a simple lesson; putting it into practice took experience. Pastors learn to be pastors by caring for congregations; evangelists have to be taught on the road. For me, the Holy Spirit school of evangelism was held on the highway.

Initiated in Orlando

Both I and the congregation of Christ the King Episcopal Church were thrown into revival and sent on the sawdust trail in one fell swoop. There was a steep learning curve. Most of us were homebodies, perfectly comfortable in the fellowship of our small family-size congregation. A traveling ministry was only a dim and distant dream until the Holy Spirit came and pushed us out the door. He sent us far beyond parochial boundaries to deliver that which we had received: a fresh anointing and the joy of the Lord.

Over time, a revival team developed, made up of myself and various members of the congregation, but the first assignment was a family affair. Even before I went to Palmetto, Fran, Elizabeth, and Hugh joined me for a one-night meeting at Ascension Church in Orlando. Father Ron Hooks and his wife, Melissa, who had attended some of the Lakeland meetings, invited us to minister at their Friday night Prayer and Praise and Holy Communion service. What happened that night surprised us as much as it did them.

The evening began in the usual way. Before the service, the pastor and musicians gathered in the kitchen, held hands, and prayed. The worship leaders petitioned for God's blessing on the service and invoked the Holy Spirit. I joined in the circle, listened, and agreed fervently with the prayers. As we prayed, the same giant weight that had pushed me to the floor on Palm Sunday pushed me to the floor again.

Was it possible to resist what revivalists of yesteryear called the "falling exercise"? Yes, I suppose it was, but it was also possible to miss God. Yielding in front of strangers was not easy, but failing to yield before God boded a worse outcome. Slowly, I sagged to the kitchen floor, letting go of the hands of those on my right and left.

Either no one seemed to notice the absence of the guest speaker, or they were just being polite by not staring. It would have been better if falling under the power was the same as fainting or blacking out into unconsciousness. At least I would not have worried about what people thought. Perhaps that was part of the exercise—learning to worry less about man's opinion and more about the Lord's intention.

While lying fully reclined on the vinyl tile floor, I was conscious of the voice of the Lord in my mind, echoing my original call. *I want you to pray for the people. Go where I tell you to go, say what I tell you to say, and pray what I tell you to pray—and no more.*

"Sure, Lord, whatever You say." I was in a kind of mental fog as I tried to focus on my assignment. Finally, with some difficulty, I pulled myself up off the floor and walked into the church.

Providing for the Unexpected

The praise and worship band sounded terrific, but the congregational singing was lackluster at best. Apparently, the Friday night crowd had their minds on everything except worship. I waited for the worship leader to admonish the congregation, but she simply plowed ahead through the list of songs. I leaned over and asked Ron if I could give an exhortation to worship. "Of course," he said. "Do whatever you like."

Stepping onto the low platform that supported the altar, I drew my index finger under my chin, signaling the band to "cut" the music. They looked a bit bewildered, wondering if something was wrong. When the musicians heard my rebuke to the congregation, however, they nodded in agreement. So far, leading worship that evening had been like pulling teeth. At the end of my exhortation, something completely spontaneous slipped out of my mouth. "If anyone would like prayer, I'll be standing over to my left."

What a strange time to pray for people! In a typical charismatic "liturgy," the pattern was fast songs, slow songs, tongues, prophesy, etc. Prayer was not offered until the end, and those who did not want to stay made a graceful exit. Praying at the beginning was confrontational. It turned out to be a road lesson: When you are in the river of God and flowing in the anointing, you must go where the river goes. What river proceeds in a straight line from the mountains to the sea? What river does not twist and turn, speed up and slow down, or rise and fall?

After my words to the congregation, the worship band began to play again, and one man came forward for prayer. He was bald and very tanned with chiseled features—a hard-looking man. Laying hands on him was like laying hands on a marble statue, and seemingly, had the same effect. It was a mini-lesson: Do not get discouraged if the first one who comes for prayer has little reaction. This was an often repeated pattern in future revival meetings. We learned to walk by faith, not by sight.

After "Marble Man," a rather plain-looking woman with a sad expression on her face came forward. As I raised my hands to pray for her, she shot backward as if hit by a blast from an airgun. There were no catchers, no ushers, and no carpet—*Bam*! The situation was repeated with a second woman before two men figured out what was happening and came forward to catch.

This was another big lesson: When flowing in the anointing, we seldom knew in advance what was going to happen. However, the Holy Spirit always knew and always provided for the unexpected. No one thought that we would need catchers, but when the need arose, helpers popped up from the congregation and solved the problem.

Stricken With Laughter

After this, the service dissolved into a quiet, holy jumble. The congregation did not storm the altar, but one by one most of them came for prayer. Soon, the entire floor was covered with people gently resting in the Spirit. The musicians played soft worship choruses in the background...and then it happened.

Somewhere far away from where I was ministering, a woman burst into laughter. It was startling, and it was loud. Those still sitting in their chairs turned to see who was causing the commotion. Waves of laughter rolled through the room as the woman chortled with great glee and clapped her hands. Rapt in joy like a baby being bounced up and down on granddaddy's knee, she did not have a care in the world or the slightest consciousness that anyone else in the room was watching or listening.

Joy began to spread throughout the congregation. The minimal reaction was a smile, but most people laughed hysterically. Even some of the "original recipe, frozen chosen, traditional types" could not keep a poker face. A few tried hard to keep an aristocratic "stiff upper lip," but they failed.

Something was decidedly different about this meeting. Episcopalians generally are not known for preaching and teaching, but they do one thing with confidence: celebrate and receive Holy Communion. That night, however, God wanted to celebrate something else. We never made it to the communion table; there was no confession of sin, no prayers of the people, no broken bread. Yet, almost everyone experienced the tangible presence of the Lord and the joy of the Holy Ghost.

It was at this time that I first really realized how much my ministry had been transformed, as if the power had increased by 100,000 volts. The transfer of the anointing that Brother Rodney had prayed for had happened, and now it was being transferred through me as I prayed for others. Ascension Church was not my first experience of ministering with a supernatural unction, but this was different, quicker, faster, and stronger.

When the curtain came down on that delightful evening, one image was unforgettable. Melissa, the pastor's wife, was the complete antithesis of an emotional charismatic. She always had it together: well organized, a fashionable dresser, an elegant home, etc. At the end of the service, Melissa was lying under the altar, pounding the carpet with her arms and kicking her feet. Her head rolled from side to side, and she was overtaken by silly laughter. "Help!" she cried, quoting from *Alice in Wonderland*, "I've fallen and I can't get up! Ha ha ha ha ha ha ha ha ha!"

This meeting in Orlando was a turning point, and my ministry was never the same afterward. The fresh anointing followed wherever I went, with signs, wonders, and miracles the order of the day. Invitations came pouring in by the dozens, and the Lord continued to teach me how to be an evangelist and how to flow in the Holy Spirit revival.

Spiritual Warfare?

The pastor of "St. Kilda's" invited me to bring a team for a two-day meeting. St. Kilda is a pseudonym, but the story is true. Two days is not much time to sow revival into a congregation, but our congregation was eager to share what we had received. Seven others from the parish went along with me to help with the music, testimonies, and catching. Our experience at St. Kilda's was a lesson in the school of hard knocks: Revival melts away pretensions, exposes sin, and demands holiness of life.

Even before we hit the highway, there was a roadblock to overcome—money. At the time, our church could not afford to field a ministry team, and St. Kilda's, which was about the same size, could not afford to pay our expenses. How could we charge for what we received at no cost? The Bible says, "Freely you have received, freely give,"[3] but who pays the bills? We needed seed money to get started.

Three weeks before our first ministry team hit the sawdust trail, I received a phone call from Solomon, a Spirit-filled man who attended a traditional church. I had known Solomon for years and had ministered to him on several occasions. "I need to make an appointment for deliverance," he said.

I had long since given up praying for every "Tom, Demon, and Harry" who rang up for counseling, but usually helped acquaintances, especially those from churches who did not believe in exorcism. The revival had further distanced us from spiritual warfare for two reasons. One, the power of the Spirit was so much greater that demons did not come around as much as formerly when we paid them so much attention. Two, since the Spirit's power was in the life of every believer as much as it was in the pastor and priest, each person was expected to take over the reigns of his or her own spiritual life.

Revival caused us to revise our view of the devil. The spiritual warfare movement had almost succeeded in elevating the evil one to a position of power rivaling that of God Himself. It had a big effect on charismatic churches, including ours. When revival came, we began to live as victorious Christians. There were no more long deliverance sessions as devils were cast out with a short, simple, powerful prayer.

"Why don't you have your pastor pray for you?" I teased Solly, showing my frustration with Spirit-filled folks like himself who continued to attend dead, mainline churches.

"You know he doesn't go in for that stuff," Solly replied.

---

3. Mt. 10:8b.

Called on the Carpet

"Why don't you come in on Sunday, say about 10:00 a.m.?" I continued to tease him, reflecting the change revival had brought in our attitude about counseling.

"But, isn't that your service time?"

"Yes. That's when the Counselor is in," I chided.

"Gee, I don't know if I could do that. Your church is way out on the north side of town, and I have to pick up Gwendoline for church. She's this girl I've been dating. And she lives all the way down on the south side. I don't know if I can make it..."

Fine, I thought, *keep your old demons. If, as a Spirit-filled Christian, you know you have demons, why don't you cast them out yourself. If you don't have enough faith to cast them out, you probably don't have enough faith to keep them out if I cast them out for you.* Of course, a proper pastor and priest would never verbalize such cruel and heartless thoughts even if they were true, but I thought them nonetheless.

"Besides," Solly continued to protest, "you need to know the background of my situation before you pray."

"Not really. The Lord knows everything," I said, lancing his final objection.

This attitude was a huge change from our pre-revival approach to deliverance ministry. In the past, we would spend hours listening to the life histories of those who came for prayer. Now we simply laid hands on the person, often with no spoken prayer at all. If we did speak, it was simply, "Greater is He who is in me, than you who are in him (or her.) Out! Now!"

Solly was not used to the change. "Well, I'll have to see," he concluded and hung up the phone. To my surprise, Solomon showed up for church alone the following Sunday and sat on the front row.

Seed Money

How do I deal tactfully with this? I thought. *Shall I give an altar call for all the demon possessed? No, they probably would not come anyway. How about a general invitation for prayer for those who have been feeling "a little oppressed"? Yeah, that should do it. Solly will take the hint and come for prayer.*

Solly did not take the hint. Instead, he remained seated, wistfully looking out the window—no small task since the church windows were frosted. Perhaps he had a spirit of X-ray vision. Finally, I walked over, grabbed him by the arm, and pulled him to his feet. "Free!" I demanded.

Solly vibrated for a few seconds and then fell over backwards. For ten minutes he lay motionless on the red carpet of the sanctuary floor. When he was able to stand, I laid hands on him again. "In Jesus name!" Down he went for another ten minutes.

Solomon came back again the following week for more prayer. After that, I did not hear from him again until the day his letter arrived in the mail—two days before our trip to St. Kilda's. I rushed into the office, anxious to get my desk cleared before departing. The parish secretary tried to stop me as I passed by her desk. "A letter came for you," she said, talking through the doorway.

"Just handle it, will you please? I'm trying to get ready for the trip."

"You may want to see this one. There's a check in it."

That halted me in my tracks. The letter was from Solomon thanking me for my ministry and saying that he was feeling much better. Enclosed was a check for $500 to be used at my discretion. There it was—the "seed money"—just what we needed to "sow" revival at St. Kilda's with no charge to them.

What a great lesson: God even provides seed money![4] We also learned a principle of faith. If you listen to God and do what He says, the money will come. Solly's check for $500 paid all our team's expenses. Neither church was out a penny. St. Kilda's received an offering for us at each service, which provided seed money to sow revival into the next church.

"Aclewistic"

It was at St. Kilda's that Gary, our praise and worship leader, coined the term *"aclewistic,"* meaning no spiritual discernment regarding revival, as in "without a clue." To be *"totally aclewistic"* meant to be completely lacking in exposure to or understanding of revival. At first, the people of St. Kilda's were "totally aclewistic."

St. Kilda's was not unusual in this regard. People were "aclewistic" almost everywhere we went, and with good reason. God sent us to places that *needed* revival. Often, our team rolled into town on "cloud nine" only to find a congregation on "cloud one." We started from scratch, teaching basic biblical truths. We quickly learned to assume nothing.

The congregation at St. Kilda's may have been "aclewistic," but they were hungry for God. We taught new songs and testified about our refreshed love for Jesus. Sometimes they stared at us, as if we were from outer space. Some even raised objections. After the evening meeting at St. Kilda's, a fractured-looking woman came up to me and expressed her disappointment. "I was expecting you to be like Francis McNutt [a well-known charismatic Roman Catholic priest]. I thought your service would be like his, but it's not. I don't like it, and I'm not coming back tomorrow."

Unsolicited criticism, we learned, came with revival territory. Old world charismatics—mainline church members who were filled

---

4.   "Now He who supplies seed to the sower and bread for food will also supply and increase your store of seed and will enlarge the harvest of your righteousness" (2 Cor. 9:10).

with the Spirit in the 1970's and 1980's—came expecting more of the same. This was a different move of God, however, with new music, a new emphasis, and a fresh anointing. Many charismatics, like the fractured woman, had a form of spiritual myopia and did not receive the revival.

We found that we needed an entire filing cabinet for the letter "P" for "Pharisee." Many Christians, even Spirit-filled ones, were unmoveable, like wax idols from previous days of glory. They rejected the fresh fire of revival and chose instead to remain frozen in another period of history—Pharisees in a lifeless wax museum.

Exposing the Wounds

The next lesson at St. Kilda's came as a huge and very sad surprise. On the second day, at the beginning of the lunch break, the pastor interrupted a conversation I was having with a man who had been at the meeting. "Would you excuse us please," he said to the man. Then looking very stiff and stern, he addressed me, "Please come this way."

My heart was in my throat as we walked toward his office. I wondered what I had said. Did I step on someone's doctrinal toes? Was the "fractured woman" a close relative? I began to prepare my apology, but instead it was the pastor who apologized.

"I am sorry this had to come up at this time," he said. "My wife and I tried our best to prevent it from coming out now. You see, we have had serious marital problems for years. We have been to counseling, but it didn't work. Can you help us?" His stern look changed to desperation as he looked at his wife, who sat pitifully on the couch in tears.

Now I was the one who was clueless. Some action was required, but what? According to my watch, there were 20 minutes left in which to have lunch and glue the couple back together well enough to finish the revival meeting. It was impossible. All I could do was pray for them and encourage them to trust God for the solution. Revival turns up the light of Christ and exposes brokenness and sin—not to condemnation, but to healing.

The surprise marriage encounter foreshadowed many future revival meetings. Sometimes whole churches erupted when buried division and hatred came to the surface. It would be easy to conclude that revival causes division and splits churches, but as one honest pastor confessed, "The division was already there. Revival simply laid it bare." When revival exposes sin, the sorrowful confess their sins and repent, while the self-righteous blame the new move of God and its leaders.[5]

None of these lessons were new revelation, yet they were new to us. Everywhere we went, people were "aclewistic," just as we had been in the beginning. We learned as we went and taught what we learned. This was especially true as the Lord opened doors for us to minister outside the walls of our own denomination.

---

5.   "And the man said, 'The woman whom Thou gavest to be with me, she gave me of the tree, and I did eat' " (Gen. 3:12 KJV).

Chapter
Ten

Out the Front Door

... "*Let us go somewhere else—to the nearby villages—so I can preach there also...* (Mark 1:38).

As denominational Christians, life was fairly routine, especially cloistered away in the Anglican castle. When revival came, it lowered the drawbridge and opened the gates. Traditional walls that separated us from the rest of the Christian family were breached as our emerging revival ministry was invited to non-Episcopal churches. This is what my wife meant when she said that the revival made her feel like "a backyard dog that's been let out the front door."

Backyard dogs, like denominational Christians, have a lot going for them. For one thing, they are always fed. The menu may not vary much, but they can look forward with confidence to someone yelling "SUPPER TIME!" The lack of variety is, at least, familiar, comfortable, and safe. Backyard dogs also have doghouses to shield them from "every wind of doctrine." If the wind gets too strong or the weather turns too cold, they are treated to a special night in the garage. Occasionally, despite the no-dogs-allowed-in-the-house rule, a backyard dog is smuggled into a child's bedroom, and if he behaves, he may spend the night.

Backyard dogs are protected. They can growl at the mailman, the U.P.S. delivery woman, and the meter reader with no retribution. While safely secured behind a wire fence, they can bark their own dogma at bigger dogs passing by.

Fran and I were backyard dogs, perfectly content in our belief that there was no better courtyard than the Anglican Communion. To stray was dangerous because the prowling dogcatcher, "Mr. E. Roneous Doctrine," lurked just beyond the fence. We did not feel imprisoned, just protected. It was a reasonable understanding, until the front door opened.

Once revival let us "out the front door," we met scores of men and women who were mighty in the Lord. They were not the hairy heretics we feared, but long lost brothers and sisters in Christ. Revival brought reunion to the Body of Christ.

Reports of revival spread rapidly, and those who knew what genuine revival was wanted it for their congregation; it did not matter who delivered it. Requests poured in from outside the Episcopal community and from people we did not know. The accounts that follow show how our revival ministry moved "out the front door."

Twenty-Twenty Bull Street

The Christian Revival Center in Savannah, Georgia, sensed that God was moving mightily in revival, bringing His glory into the midst of His people. Pastors Ron and Rosie Chambers invited a team from our congregation to come to their church. It was our first visit to a nondenominational congregation, and the first time that our services were advertised as "Revival Meetings." Ron Chambers, a student of revival, had read the handwritten letters of John Wesley in the Savannah public library. So when I asked him to describe what the past revivals were like, I expected something profound—a penetrating historical insight.

"Revivals are loud and messy—downright boisterous and tumultuous. They are upsetting to some and offensive to others."

Ron's answer disappointed me. I had wanted to hear that revivals were holy, sanctifying, and reverent, and a time for renewal of sound doctrine and church growth—anything besides "loud and messy." Yet, strangely enough, Ron's research matched perfectly with our experience. We had to accept the fact that our new ministry was exporting a loud, messy, and tumultuous move of God.

The Christian Revival Center was located at 2020 Bull Street. Somehow, I found making our revival debut on "Bull Street" particularly funny. I was still adjusting to being introduced as an "evangelist," a title of ill repute among many in my denomination. To me, "Revival Meeting on Bull Street" sounded like the title of a Broadway comedy.

It was not a prestigious address. The original Presbyterian congregation had long since departed, and the neighborhood around the church, rife with drug dealing and shootings, was called by many "the war zone."

By contrast, pastors Ron and Rosie, tired of their heavily administrative duties, had resigned their 350-member suburban church in order to start a new church in the city where they could be more involved with hands-on ministry. The "war zone" was the perfect place to find needy people. The idea of ministering in the "war zone" was appealing to our ministry team as well. Good News and changed lives were desperately needed on Bull Street.

My family and I stayed with an old friend from seminary, known affectionately by our children as "Miss Bunny." Miss Bunny lived with her roommate Sophie in downtown Savannah in a house filled with fine furniture, antiques, and oil paintings. Sophie was a beautiful, elegant, black, standard-size poodle whose boisterous behavior in such formal, staid surroundings made her the perfect paradigm of revival. Her irrepressible energy brought life and joy to the formal, charming art museum in which she lived.

Miss Bunny, a believer at heart, had not been much of a church-goer since her divorce from her clergyman husband. Fran and I did not expect her to attend the revival services and did not plan to force the issue. So we were completely surprised when she walked into the Friday night service. The very loud bang, boom, rock 'n' roll, Holy Ghost music was in keeping with Pastor Ron's first principle of revival: Revival was noisy. *Miss Bunny won't put up with this for long*, I thought; but for some reason, she stayed and looked genuinely interested in the proceedings.

An Overwhelming Response

As a novice evangelist, I immediately made a mess of things. Early in the service, right after the music stopped, I offered prayer for anyone who felt a desperate need. I had the impression that there were one or two sick people, and I had seen one very old man who was unlikely to stay for a four-hour meeting. To my shock and dismay, 250 people—almost the entire congregation—came forward.

People poured down the aisles in a flood: Musicians put down their instruments, children ran forward, and old folks hobbled to the front for a blessing. The only problem was that there was no room to pray for that many at one time. Members of the revival team lined the people up and tried to sort out the chaos. We learned that everyone has a need that is urgent to them.

Before I had laid hands on a dozen people, a loud booming sound reverberated through the room. It was so startling that I jumped, and several other people gasped involuntarily. My first thought was that part of the building had collapsed. Actually, a very obese woman at the far end of the prayer line had fallen back-ward, hitting her head as she landed. The sound was amplified by the sanctuary's hardwood floors vibrating like a drum over the basement below.

For a few breathless moments, all ministry stopped as members of the congregation rushed to her assistance. As she lay motionless on the oak wood floor, I assumed she was dead. Apparently, she had fallen spontaneously; as I had laid hands on one end of the line, she had fallen out on the other. My heart was still pounding out of my chest when she eventually regained her composure and sat up, completely unhurt, and perplexed by all the attention. I had never really believed the old Pentecostal saying, "If it is really from the Holy Ghost, no one will be hurt," but I could not explain this any other way.

As my fear subsided and I began to think more rationally, I realized that this was Pastor Ron's second principle of revival perfectly illustrated: Revival was messy. What could be messier than having folks "slain in the Spirit" when no one was praying for them and there were no catchers? Most church services are at the least orderly. Could it be that the order of God, at least in terms of revival, appears messy to the narrow mind of man?

The biggest surprise of the evening was yet to come. Near the end of the prayer time, Miss Bunny descended the aisle and stood in the prayer line. My heart sank just a bit. *What if I pray for her and nothing happens? Will she think it's all a hoax? Will it confirm her worst suspicions about false religion in the church?* It could endanger our friendship. *Come on, God!* I prayed silently as I laid hands on her. *Here is Your chance to give Miss Bunny a blessing.*

My mouth dropped open when, in very ladylike fashion, Miss Bunny toppled over just like everyone else. I could scarcely believe it. I was ecstatic, jumping up and down on the inside. *Wow*, I thought, *this is real revival! Miss Bunny would not feign a swoon in front of hundreds of strangers and certainly not at 2020 Bull Street!*

Later that evening, Miss Bunny commented on her experience, "Well, I'll say one thing. You didn't push me. I don't envy you. This stuff is very powerful, and you have a huge responsibility. You had better be careful and not let this go to your head." It was good advice from a wise woman.

Praying for the Mayor

Very early the next morning (*too* early for an evangelist who had conducted services late into the night), I attended the Mayor's Prayer Breakfast, which was held at the church. Something as mundane as politicians at prayer did not appeal to me, but it was important to Pastor Ron because he had a vision to "take Savannah for Jesus."

However, the mayor surprised me in several ways. First, in a far cry from Savannah's "good old boys" and southern gentlemen, the mayor was a woman. Second, she was Jewish and originally from New York. Third, and most surprising of all to me, she actually prayed. In 20 years of ministry and attending prayer breakfasts, I had never heard a politician pray; that was usually left up to the professional clergy. This mayor did it herself. "God, we want the drug dealers off the streets of our city. We want Savannah to be a safe place for our children to grow up. And God, we need Your help to do it."

After breakfast, Ron introduced me to the mayor, who asked me to pray that she would have the wisdom to solve the city's problems.

"I'll pray for wisdom," I answered, "but there is something else you need." My words were not my own; they came from somewhere else. "You not only need wisdom, you need power. May I also pray that God will give you the power to do the job?"

She agreed, gave me a firm handshake, and bowed her head. At the end of my prayer, she echoed, "Amen!"

The revival at 2020 Bull Street was a real learning experience for us. Like so many other occasions when we prayed for people,

134

we never heard about the result and rarely knew if we were laying a foundation or building on one that was already in place. Yet our faith was never higher, and we knew that the Lord was leading us and teaching us to obey. It also reminded us that people are the same everywhere. We all have needs that are urgent to us—needs that may be carried to a God who is more willing to give than we are to receive.

Seed Money for Drums

The next trip out of our backyard was to St. Simon's Island, Georgia. Nativity Episcopal teamed up with The Christian Renewal Center (CRC) to invite us for an entire week. For our fledgling revival team, the services were a watershed event—the first time we held a week-long series of meetings. Beginning on Sunday, we met day and night, through Friday. Morning attendance ranged from 50 to 75, and the evenings from 100 to 300. Our newly launched ministry continued to develop with an increase in signs and wonders.

Fran drove up for the Thursday evening service, taking Elizabeth and Hugh out of school for Friday. I asked her to say a few words, but she was reluctant. When, on rare occasions, she agreed to speak at a women's meeting, she fretted about it and prepared for days, reading the Bible and making copious notes. Extemporaneous speaking was not her style, but that night the Spirit prompted her and she agreed to speak. "I could give my testimony," she said, "maybe five minutes max."

As Fran began to speak, I was stunned. This was not the same demure, conservative woman I had been married to for almost 20 years. She shouted, stomped her foot, and pointed her finger in the air like Aimee Semple McPherson. She preached, pleaded, and exhorted the congregation for almost 20 minutes; and when she was finished, they applauded.

Applause was not the only affirmation Fran received. During the meeting, an envelope with Fran's name on it was put in the offering plate. Inside was a check made out to her for $1,000.

Before the revival, that money probably would have turned into a shopping trip. Instead, after we returned home, Fran "sowed" the money, contributing every penny to the church to establish a fund for the purchase of a set of drums. This was in response to a recommendation from our bishop after he visited our radically changed congregation for the first time. He had found that drums had greatly enhanced the worship music of the Virginia church he had previously served, and believed that the same would be true for us.

It was the best "godly admonition" I ever received from a bishop. Fran's first love offering established the fund. Not long after, an old friend visiting the church heard about the drum fund and contributed another $500—the exact balance needed to buy the drums.

What Do You Do With a Drunken Sailor?

On another night at the St. Simon's revival, 15 crew members from the Mercy Ship, *S. S. Hope* attended the meeting. Affiliated with Youth With a Mission (YWAM), the medical missionary and outreach ship for young people was docked across the river in Brunswick, Georgia. Its young Christian staff, who came from West Africa, the Dominican Republic, and the U.S., were from an evangelical background with little or no personal experience of the Holy Spirit.

I wondered what would happen if the missionaries received the fresh anointing. Would they be quarantined when they went back aboard ship? Would some Calvinistic Captain Bligh make them walk the plank? Was it fair to pray for these brothers and sisters from another dimension of Christianity? Or, was it unfair to withhold the blessing that we ourselves had received and been commissioned to share? Like so many of our other questions, these soon became irrelevant when the Lord whispered to me, *Pray for them.*

"I want to pray for all the missionaries," I said. A dozen teenagers sheepishly made their way to the front, embarrassed by the cheering, clapping, whistling congregation. Without any further prompting, the 12 held hands, giggled a bit, and lined up across the front of the church. When I laid hands on them, however, there was no response. Were they indoctrinated, somehow inoculated against the Spirit's touch? No, they were just inexperienced. They needed a little time and more personal ministry. Like so many others we prayed for, they needed to be taught how to receive.

I began to minister intuitively and asked them to break the chain of hands—to let go of one another and lift their hands to the Lord. Not that this was any sort of magical posture, but I wanted them to be free to focus on Jesus without being distracted by touching or being touched by someone else.

As I was now able to pray for individuals rather than a whole group, one by one, they began to receive. First, a tall girl in the middle of the prayer line began to convulse and chuckle. Second, a handsome young African man began to laugh uncontrollably. Their companions looked on in amazement as the young mariners began to yield. Soon, almost all were laughing, staggering, and falling on the floor, intoxicated and exhilarated with the Spirit. It was like the Day of Pentecost revisited when bystanders thought the disciples were drunk on new wine.[1] We should have sung, "What do you do with a drunken sailor?" or prayed that they would not be thrown into the brig when they went back to the ship. Instead, the congregation joined in the rapturous rejoicing.

We never learned their names or discovered what happened to them, but the experience with the missionaries explained a prophecy the Lord gave on the night I was called to be an evangelist: "You will touch hundreds, thousands, and millions...."

---

1.   See Acts 2:13.

"Hundreds" and "thousands" were conceivable...but "millions"? How could it be?

If, as in the case of the Mercy Ship crew, the anointing that passed to us was also passed through us, millions were easily imaginable. If even a few of the 12 young missionaries received the fresh anointing and passed it on at each port of call, it could spread inland and touch millions.

Holy Rolling

The final night of the St. Simon's revival made the biblical description of Pentecost seem tame in comparison. The worship was so exuberant and the anointing so strong that people were spontaneously slipping out of their chairs. Laughter turned to howling. Some shrieked while others jumped for joy. Heaven came down and swallowed the meeting.

I have always resented the term *Holy Roller*, especially when it has been applied to me by my fellow priests. It was their way of implying that I was not a true Episcopalian—the "thinking man's religion"—but an anti-intellectual, emotional Pentecostal. However, in light of this final service on St. Simon's, it looked as if they might be right after all.

It was about midnight when the holy rolling began. The congregation had thinned to about 100 people, and the chairs had been stacked against the walls to leave more open floor space. The Spirit's intensity remained strong. There were a few jumpers and shakers and a few others who lay swooned. Then, almost unnoticed, a man began to roll.

He was short, bald, and about 40 years old. Face down on the carpeted floor with his hands clasped behind his neck and his legs straight, he suddenly rolled several times to his right, flip-flop, flip-flop, flip-flop, as if a giant spatula were turning pancakes on a grill.

The movement caught our attention, and we were tempted to stop him, fearing he might cause someone to fall. However, whenever he came to an obstacle, like a person or a wall, he stopped. We knew this was supernatural because his elbows covered his eyes and he could not see a thing. After he stopped, he rolled in the opposite direction back to where he had started. Then he was off again, moving to his left. By now everyone in the room had stopped to watch.

Finally, as if by intention, he rolled into a woman who lay "slain" on the floor. *Bang!* With her eyes still closed, and without speaking, she too began to roll. Unlike the gentleman, she rolled with her arms extended straight over her head in haphazard fashion like a paint roller coating a wall.

With no apparent connection to rollers one and two, a tall, lanky teenage boy in the back of the room began to roll. It seemed that it was not so much that he himself was rolling, but that he was being rolled by an unseen blast of air. It was completely involuntary, and in his embarrassment, he laughed uncontrollably, gripping his stomach as he tried to restrain himself.

After ten minutes or so, both the woman and the teenager stopped rolling, but the bald man continued to roll from one end of the room to the other, picking up velocity with each pass.

Instead of amusement, a sense of awe settled upon us as we realized that we really were in the presence of the Lord. At the same time, my intellect tried to defend itself by posing some logical questions. *Has this man lost his mind? Is he an escaped mental patient, or is he having a nervous breakdown? Am I having a nervous breakdown?* Finally, I turned to the pastor and asked, "Do you know this man?"

"Yes," he said in his soft, slow southern drawl, "he is the principal of the local elementary school."

My jaw dropped open. This was astounding, incredible, beyond belief. Perhaps that was the whole point. God was giving us a sign of His omnipotence. Despite what some believe, He is still in charge of creation, is still in charge of the Church, and is still reaching down from Heaven to touch the lives of His saints.

Going Full-Time

In the late summer of 1994, while conducting a revival meeting in the southwestern U.S., the Lord called me full-time to the ministry of revival and evangelism. At the same time, my church board, who had formerly approved my dual ministry, changed their minds and expressed their desire to have a full-time pastor, instead of a traveling priest. Before we were able to work everything out, however, Fran and I left for a three-week crusade in Africa, where we continued to finalize the details of my resignation from Christ the King Episcopal Church. On October 31, I resigned via fax. My new full-time ministry began the following day, All Saints Day, November 1, 1994, in Cape Town, South Africa.

The irony is that I had never wanted to go to Africa. When I was a boy, a cousin of mine named Burleigh Law, a Methodist lay missionary, was shot and killed by revolutionaries in the Belgian Congo. As a result, out of fear of going to Africa, I grew up with an aversion to becoming a serious Christian. The Lord had other plans.

Another irony is that my first excursion as a full-time evangelist would put me in a very unlikely place for a signs and wonders revival—a Dutch Reformed church. What would happen if a restorative move of the Holy Spirit invaded the traditions, rites, and rituals of a denominational church? Could a traditional, historic church receive revival fire without burning to ashes? What would happen if there were a fire in *this* wax museum? As it turned out, everything about the revival meeting at Tableview Dutch Reformed Church, Cape Town, South Africa, was so unlikely that only the God of "no impossibilities" could have done it.

Crossing Barriers

Our South African tour began at the Maranatha Fellowship in Cape Town. Afterward, we moved across the city for a week-long revival at Good Hope Christian Centre. Good Hope met in a brand-new, 3,000-seat, warehouse-style venue in an industrial area. On Sunday morning, 1,500 worshipers gathered to sing and dance to the driving, rhythmic music of a 60-member, multicultural praise band. The band, like the congregation, was a mixture of black, white, and colored South Africans, as well as Indians and other Asians.

Sunday evening church attendance rose to 2,000. Volkswagen vans arrived at the church with a dozen-plus people jammed into them. Some came from 50 miles away, and many traveled over an hour, walking from their homes to the closest towns, taking taxis to the train station, and then coming the rest of the way by rail. For many, it was a great sacrifice just to come to the church; and when the music started, the whole congregation became extraordinarily focused on God. They came for healing, deliverance, and salvation and brought friends and family with them to receive the same. The worship was nothing short of glorious as eyes closed, hands rose, and feet danced. Monday night was the same.

On Tuesday morning I received a call from Derrick, the assistant pastor at the church, asking if I would speak at another congregation, Tableview Dutch Reformed Church, on the other side of the city. I declined without giving it much thought. "Why can't the people from Tableview drive across town and come to the meetings at Good Hope?"

"For two reasons," Derrick explained. "First, there's a social barrier. Tableview is an affluent neighborhood, and people from there do not come to our side of town. Second, there's an ecclesiastical barrier. Mainline church members don't mix with Pentecostals. We always invite them to come when we have an international speaker, but they never cross the line."

This was not too surprising, considering that Good Hope was in a tough neighborhood near St. Andrew's Anglican Church, where gunmen had massacred the congregation before Nelson Mandela became president. As a result, 40 armed guards were present for every church service at Good Hope, 8 of whom were on the platform. Ecclesiastical apartheid was no surprise either. It is much the same in the United States, where mainline churchmen are undeniably prejudiced against Pentecostals.

Despite these reasons, I still declined. Good Hope had invited me for a full week, and I was enjoying the ministry there.

Wednesday morning they tried again. Derrick informed me that a group of Methodists, Baptists, Anglicans, and Dutch Reformed wanted me to speak at their joint service that very evening. I still resisted, believing that if traditional church members were not motivated enough to overcome their narrow-mindedness and drive across town, they would probably not receive revival either. Besides that, there was the question of who would take the service at Good Hope.

When Derrick suggested that Fran could lead the service, Fran frantically indicated to me that there was *no way* she would do it. Fran had never led a service before. Once again, I declined and hung up.

Five minutes later, the phone rang again. This time it was Wendy, the pastor's wife, a very talented and persuasive woman. She asked me to reconsider. "We have been trying to build bridges to these people for years without much success. We hate to miss this opportunity. It is very unusual. Do you think Fran might reconsider too?"

Her argument convinced me, and Fran agreed on the condition that she would give her testimony and pray for people, but someone else would lead the worship, take the offering, and give the altar call. With these conditions accepted, the unlikely deal was done. Now it was my turn to have cold feet. Would revival fire burn in a Dutch oven?

Fire in a Dutch Oven

The Dutch Reformed Church was the church of the Afrikaners—the establishment, the elite. Until the election of Nelson Mandela, it was the church of the ruling white minority and had laid the theological foundations for apartheid. Only recently had the Church recanted that position. Theologically, the Church was conservative, Calvinistic, and very traditional.

Derrick picked me up at the hotel an hour before the service, and when we arrived at the Tableview Church, we were introduced to the Dutch Reformed pastors. Dominees, as they are called, are well educated, spending seven years in theological training. Derrick and I also met and greeted the pastors from the Anglican, Methodist, and Baptist churches. The dominee at Tableview, Philip Botha, was leading the music rehearsal with his guitar. Eventually, he came over and introduced himself and Mrs. Botha.

While the pastors visited, a crowd of 350 gathered in the church, filling it to capacity. They were well-dressed, polite, and reserved in their manner. Tableview Dutch Reformed was different from Good Hope Christian Centre in every way: geographically, sociologically, theologically, and liturgically. I was heartened by the attendance, but I wondered how they would receive the fresh anointing.

The service began with early charismatic, slow worship choruses sung to a rhythm guitar. For all their enthusiasm, the congregation might as well have sung hymns. A Pentecostal platitude about the glory of God echoed in my ears. "You can praise it down, preach it down, or pray it down." I usually relied on praise and worship to get things cooking, but tonight looked like a "preach-it-down" night.

After the music and offering, it was my turn. The congregation sat bolt upright in their seats, so stiff and formal that they looked almost like cardboard cutouts. Nevertheless, I was determined to engage them. I taught, testified, exhorted, preached, and told stories and humorous anecdotes, but there was almost no reaction—barely a smile or grin. *Maybe a responsive reading will draw them out.* I shouted, "Blessed are those who hunger and thirst for righteousness, for they shall be..."

"...filled," came the muffled response from ten people. *Well, that's that,* I thought. *Maybe Derrick and I can make it back in time to catch the end of the service at Good Hope.* I decided to offer prayer for anyone who wanted it, and then close the meeting.

Surprisingly, 25 people, including some of the pastors, responded to the call for prayer. They queued up across the front in a perfectly straight line, and as I prayed, fell to the floor just the same as at any other meeting.

The action picked up, and I became more attentive to what the Lord was doing. When the floor at the front of the church was full, I prayed for people in the aisles and cross-aisles. Almost everyone in the whole congregation came for prayer and fell silently to the ground.

Even the musicians stopped playing and came for prayer. Accustomed to background music during prayer ministry, I was a little uncomfortable with the silence. Suddenly, a woman lying on the floor in the front of the church broke the stillness with bubbling laughter that quickly became a shriek, causing everyone to look in her direction. Smiles cracked the conservative veneer on the stoic faces, and joyful electricity began to charge the atmosphere with expectation.

Without any encouragement, the laughter spread. Contagious germs of joy infected one after another until the sanctuary was holy bedlam. Some rocked back and forth as they lay on the floor. Others rolled slowly, involuntarily. One man became quite agitated

and cried out, "I'm hot...I'm burning hot...I'm on *fire!*" A fashion-
ably dressed young woman lying in the aisle to my left caught my
attention as she thrashed back and forth, rolling from side to side.
She slammed into a pew, reversed herself and rolled into the
opposite pew. Her gyrations were so violent I was concerned for
her safety.

Just above her, standing at the top of the aisle, was her dominee, his green eyes and prominent brow analyzing her every
action. In heavily accented English with a tinge of amazement he
said, "Das ist da quietest voman in my kerk" (That is the quietest
woman in my church).

Amazement was also my reaction. I understood that God
could lay people out in a Pentecostal church in America, or even
leave them giggling at Good Hope...but in a Dutch Reformed
church? That had to be Holy Ghost fire in a wax museum. Neither
denomination nor theology, neither language nor liturgy impeded
the Holy Spirit, and nothing, it seemed, could prevent hungry people from receiving a fresh touch from Heaven. The Flame that
ignited the Protestant Reformation had come once again to
reform and burn the Church back to its roots.

Chapter Eleven

Episcopal Fire

"Once more I will shake not only the earth but also the heavens." The words "once more" indicate the removing of what can be shaken—that is, created things—so that what cannot be shaken may remain (Hebrews 12:26b-27).

Just as God is no respecter of persons,[1] revival is no respecter of denominations. Our revival ministry has witnessed the fire of God fall among Methodists, Baptists, Catholics, Presbyterians, Pentecostals, and charismatic churches. Reviews have been mixed among the members of our own Episcopal communion, but even there, the flames of revival have touched the hearts of people. I want to share with you two revival meetings in Episcopal churches that well describe the effect of fresh fire in the "wax museum Anglicanus." These examples also reveal the forces that open and close the door to the fresh wind of revival.

---

1.   See Acts 10:34 KJV.

The Devil's Millhopper

Our first full-blown, six-day, morning-and-evening revival in an Episcopal church was in April, 1994 at St. Michael's Church in Gainesville, Florida. St. Mike's was located on the corner of NW 34ᵗʰ Street and 23ʳᵈ Avenue, an intersection known as the "Devil's Millhopper" because of its proximity to a natural funnel-shaped hole in the earth. Judging from the responses at this meeting, we made the devil "hopping mad."

I had first met the Reverends Joan and Lou Mattia three years previously at a charismatic spiritual warfare conference. At the time, they had just accepted a call to be copastors at St. Michael's. I had never heard of "copastors," and I told them it would not work, but they proved me wrong. When they invited me to come for a week-long revival, I accepted without hesitation. Several weeks later, however, I was rethinking my decision. Joan and Lou had not been to the Lakeland Revival, and I wanted to make sure they understood that this was a new move of God and very different from "charismatic renewal."

I asked Bob, the parishioner at my church who served as our revival administrator, to set up a meeting with the Mattias as soon as possible. Within a few days, we made the two-and-a-half-hour drive up to Gainesville to discuss the meetings. "We should not alarm them unnecessarily," I told Bob, "but I want them to know that revival turns churches upside down. Let's tell them what happened at our church and see how they react. We'll look them in the eye and if they flinch, we won't go."

This was a serious concern. If the Mattias were not hungry for a fresh touch from God, we would be wasting our time and theirs. An old charismatic maxim said, "A pastor cannot bring renewal, but he can stop it." The same was true of revival. If pastors are not *personally* hungry and ready to let God change them as well as their parishioners, they will never run with the new move of God. No shepherd can lead his flock anywhere that he himself is unwilling to go.

Bob agreed with my conclusions. As we pulled into the church parking lot, we paused a moment, took a deep breath, and sighed to relieve the nervous tension we felt. It wasn't as though we were about to close a business deal. We knew we were offering a gift with value beyond measure, but were unsure how it would be received. *We* knew the benefits and blessings, as well as the risks. *We* knew there was a price to be paid. The question was, would the Mattias be willing to pay it?

Reluctant but Hungry

Joan and Lou welcomed us warmly and ushered us into their office. After introductions and a few pleasantries, I was straight-forward with them about what had happened in our parish. I told them how every Sunday for weeks the Lord had laid me out on the floor in front of the whole congregation, how embarrassing it was for me, and the difficult time I had giving up control. I told them how I had finally protested to the Lord and how the Lord had silenced me with the admonition, *If you don't yield, they won't yield.*

I watched closely to gauge Joan's and Lou's reactions. If the shepherds do not yield to God, neither will the sheep. Behind his beard and eyeglasses, Lou's face was hard to read, although his blue eyes sparkled with a curious but cautious excitement. His expression reminded me of a contestant on the TV quiz show *Jeopardy* who has just hit the "Daily Double" and is considering how much to wager.

Joan spoke first. "We have been here three years, and things are finally beginning to settle down. Those people who could not adjust to "copastors" or to a female priest have left. I have worked hard to polish up the liturgy. The acolytes are trained. The organist knows when to play the service music...I'm not sure I can give all that up. Being the parish's first woman priest is difficult. I've worked hard to establish a professional image. I'm not sure I can fall out on the floor in front of the whole congregation." Lou echoed her feelings.

These were just the kind of responses that I did *not* want to hear. Joan and Lou were a little fearful, a little reluctant, and a little reserved. As pastors, they wanted revival for their congregation, but were not sure they could yield to it themselves. Over the next few years, I learned that the Mattias' attitudes were characteristic of almost all pastors. They had the same feelings and reservations that I had once had. Shepherds are reluctant to be personally vulnerable in front of their flocks. They cherish a pastoral scene—sheep in repose in green pastures, drinking from still waters with their souls yielded to God—but yielding themselves...?

Still, I came away with a positive feeling about the meetings at St. Michael's. The Mattias' honesty outweighed their reluctance, and they had a genuine desire for a move of God. It was evidence of their love for their flock. Bob and I both felt we had a thumbs-up from the copastors as well as from the Lord.

Dissenter in the Ranks

A few weeks later, revival broke out at St. Michael's. It was really something to see the fire of God blaze in such a traditional church setting. St. Mike's had long African mahogany pews anchored to a black slate floor. An immense carving of Jesus as High Priest and King, the Christus Rex, hung from cables, suspended over the stone altar. Votive candles near the side altar twinkled in crimson glass.

A remarkable cross section of people came to the meetings. Students from the nearby University of Florida, pastors from hundreds of miles away, and the saints from almost every denomination flocked to St. Michael's day and night. The First Assembly of God pastor and his wife attended every meeting, even helping to lead the singing in the mornings. By Thursday night, 50 different congregations were represented. For the first time in recent memory, St. Michael's was filled to capacity—more than 350 people.

Episcopal Fire

The meetings were a tremendous success, despite a rocky start. On Sunday night, the very first day of the revival, the spirit of the service was disrupted by a hair-raising interruption that frightened everyone. The praise and worship was over, and I was teaching about the Welsh Revival when a young man wearing a baseball cap stood up and shouted, "Can I ask a question?" His abruptness startled everyone.

Something in his tone of voice did not ring true with me. "No, you may not ask a question now," I replied. "You are welcome to stay, but you are not welcome to interrupt the meeting." My heart beat faster, an adrenaline reaction to the immanent confrontation. It quickly became evident that he had indeed come to disrupt the meeting.

The protester kept screaming. The slate floor enlivened the church acoustics and caused his shouts to reverberate throughout the building. With no idea to whom I was speaking, I said, "Please remove the gentleman from the church." Stunned silence fell across the room.

On the opposite side of the church from the protester sat a short, stocky, bulldog of a man. The "bulldog," who was enjoying the service, took the order to remove the dissident as a personal directive. Bolting across the room, he grabbed the young man and pinned his arm behind his back. A scuffle ensued, knocking over one of the band's monitor speakers with a crash.

Lou Mattia and the Assembly of God pastor both rushed over and tried to reason with the young man, but he did not listen and continued his futile attempt to escape the "bulldog's" hammer-lock. An off-duty police officer joined the impromptu "S.W.A.T. team" and forced the dissenter down the center aisle and out the front door of the church. The police officer thought the disturbance was over when, at his strong suggestion, the protester walked away. The next morning, however, Lou discovered that the church's electrical transformer had been smashed in an apparent attempt to cause a blackout.

Inside the church, the congregation was upset. A curtain of fear hung over the meeting. Sixteen years of pastoral experience told me that there were a variety of feelings about the disturbance. Some would be glad the bum was thrown out—justice had been served. Others were worried about "the one lost sheep." We prayed for the protester, then worshiped for another half hour in order to dispel the fear.

After the meeting, Joan brought me a piece of paper that had been dropped by the protester during the scuffle. The list of questions on it made his complaint easy to understand. He was a cessationist—one who believed that signs, wonders, and miracles *ceased* to exist after the New Testament period. Had we known at the time more about the history of revival, this young man's response would have been predictable. Resistance to revival comes most often from *within* the Church.

Raised From the Dead

Two nights later, an amazing thing happened to another young man, an indisputable sign and wonder. A student from the university was "raised from the dead." He was not dead in the medical sense, as in need of resuscitation. He fell under the power of the Spirit and then, in the same supernatural way, was raised again to his feet.

The young man had come to the meeting with his roommate. When it was time for testimonies, he stepped forward and told of his recent conversion. A peculiar spiritual buzz was in the atmosphere that evening, and I tried to discern what it was. Meanwhile, and typical of a new convert, the student rambled on with his new profession of faith. When I prayed for him to be baptized in the Spirit, he spoke in tongues, fell backward, and lay "slain" on the cold stone floor.

The service continued with the invitation to receive Jesus Christ, and I forgot about the young man who had "dropped out of sight"—until he interrupted the altar call. Right in the middle of the offer of salvation, at the most solemn moment of all, he emerged from nowhere. I did not see him walk up, and with good reason. He did not "walk up," he literally "rose up" from the floor!

"What happened?" he blurted out. "How did I get here?" He was genuinely bewildered.

At first, I thought it was another distraction, like the protester on the first night. "What do you mean?" I asked reluctantly, not wanting to encourage another long witness.

"Something picked me up. I was lying over there," he said, pointing to a place on the floor. "Then, suddenly, something pulled me to my feet." A dozen people sitting on the front row were nodding in agreement, confirming the sign with gestures and expressions of awe.

What appeared to be a distraction was actually a demonstration of the power of God. Sometimes God must distract us from routine religious rites, even the rite of altar calls, to turn our eyes upon Him. The arrow found its mark that night and captured our attention. Following this "raising," we had the largest altar call response of the entire week.

Our revival team relearned an old lesson at St. Michael's: Signs, wonders, and miracles confirm the resurrection of Jesus.[2] He was not merely a teacher or a prophet. He is no longer on the cross or buried in a tomb. He is more than resurrected; Jesus is

---

2. "This salvation, which was first announced by the Lord, was confirmed to us by those who heard Him. God also testified to it by signs, wonders and various miracles, and gifts of the Holy Spirit distributed according to His will" (Heb. 2:3b-4).

sitting on the *throne in Heaven*, ruling and continuing to reveal Himself through the Holy Spirit[3] in signs, wonders, and miracles.[4]

The faith of Joan and Lou Mattia was strengthened during the revival, and as it turned out, they needed it. They indeed paid a high price for revival. Over the year following the meetings, 200 people left the church, yet the church's income remained the same. Their bishop, a former pastor of St. Michael's, was less than supportive of their ministry and of the revival. At one point, they became discouraged enough to think about resigning, but stayed because they knew that the Lord did not want them to leave.

Over the next few years, the attendance at St. Mike's grew back to its pre-revival level. Unlike many pastors, the Mattias did not back off but continued to flow in the revival river. The early service, like ours at Christ the King, continued to be traditional, but the 10:30 a.m. service left room for the Spirit to move. Five years later, a contractor noticed the commercial value of their property and offered to buy it for three million dollars or to exchange it for a new facility built to their specifications in a developing area of Gainesville.

Super Bowl Sunday

How could anyone overlook the biggest Sunday on the secular calendar? Being clueless is excusable, but accepting an invitation to Nashville, Tennessee on January 29, 1995 was certainly madness! No red-blooded American in his or her right mind starts a series of church meetings on Super Bowl Sunday. Even people who do not like football watch the professional championship. Millions of people all over the world tune in to see this game of games.

That year, the rival teams were the San Francisco 49ers and the San Diego Chargers. The two California teams were playing in

3.   See Jn. 16:13-15.
4.   See Heb. 2:4.

Miami, and kickoff was set for 7:00 p.m.—the same time as our first meeting at St. Bartholomew's Episcopal Church.

Pastor Ian Montgomery was an Englishman and a long-range planner. He had invited us nine months in advance for a two-week meeting. At the time, no one thought about the Super Bowl, and although it can be argued that Christianity is not a religion, the same cannot be said about American football. For sports fans, the Super Bowl is Christmas, Easter, and Pentecost rolled into one.

I arrived at the church that first night expecting the worst. *No one will be at church on Super Bowl night!* Even if a few football-haters straggled in, the service would finish early. *At least I'll be back at the hotel in time to see the end of the game!* During the Welsh Revival, sporting events were canceled because everyone was at church. That was not likely to happen in Nashville, Tennessee...but it did. When time came for the service to begin, 300 people had packed into St. Bartholomew's!

Singing in the Rain

Just as at St. Michael's, the meetings at St. Bartholomew's were held morning and evening, Sunday through Friday. During one of the morning services, a sudden anticipation filled the air. We sensed the forthcoming of prophecy, and a hush fell over the crowd. We waited patiently and quietly. Then, from a point halfway back in the sanctuary, came the sound of a woman singing to a nursery rhyme melody: "La la la la la la."

Jesus, help us, I thought. *Just when things were getting off to a good start, a spiritual fruitloop sings a prophetic lullaby!* The dark-haired woman was in her late 30's and was sitting at the end of her row. I walked back to her and tried to subdue her with my presence, but she ignored me. "La la la la la la la. La la la la la la la. La la la la la la la," she continued to sing, as if she were rocking a baby.

It was then that I heard the Lord's voice: *Listen!*

Come on, God, give me a break. I'm in charge of the service, and if I don't put a stop to prophetess "Mother Goose," people won't respect me. Even as I argued with God, I knew I would not win.

Listen, He said, *just listen.*

What are we in for now? I wondered.

"La la la la la la la, come on out. Come on out and play with me. Come on out. Come on out and play with me. It's raining. It's raining. It's raining. Come on out and play in the rain with me." Prophetess Goose continued giggling and peeking out from under her dark hair as if to say she could not believe what she was singing either. Everyone waited politely to see what would happen.

A thunderbolt of revelation hit the congregation all at once, and they began to laugh as the interpretation broke into their consciousness. God the Father had come to play with His children! He was singing to us, beckoning us to come out and play in the refreshing rain. It was an unbelievable, unmistakable revelation. The Father, like earthly fathers, longed for intimacy with His children!

According to Rick Joyner of Morning Star Ministries in Charlotte, North Carolina, the laughter that has characterized this current revival is God's way of telling us not to take ourselves too seriously. In the same way, this woman's singing was a prophetic invitation for us to come out of our all too serious religion and play with our Father in the refreshing rain of His Spirit.

Nashville Cats

One of the things I dreamed about in Nashville was finding the perfect praise and worship leader to take on the road—a genuine "Nashville Cat." Surely Music City had an abundance of talented Christians who were looking for a great gig. At first, we were surprised by the tempo of the worship music. St. Bartholomew's was one of the most well-organized churches that we visited, and they had arranged for different Christian bands to play each night. After being in revival meetings with rollicking Pentecostal bands, to me the Nashville sound seemed very s-l-o-w.

One night, a musician was leading the congregation in singing, "We Bring the Sacrifice of Praise into the House of the Lord." The tempo was close to that of the "Blue Danube." I slipped away from the platform and walked to the back of the church and spoke to Ian Montgomery. "Does the worship leader always play this song that slowly?"

"That's Kirk Dearman," he said. "He wrote it."

Well, file that one under "different strokes for different folks." We learned another precept: Revival follows no pattern. It is not dependent on the music, the preaching, the building, or the denomination. It only depends on God's giving and our receiving.

Click-whir, Click-whir, Click-whir

Pastor Ian surprised me by inviting the local newspaper to cover the services. They came during the second week. One morning during the praise and worship, I heard the *click-whir* of a 35mm camera with an automatic film advance. It was the unmistakable sound of an expensive camera of the type that professional photographers use. Out of the corner of my eye, I spotted the scruffy-looking sharpshooter so I slipped out of the worship to confront him.

"Excuse me. Do you have permission to take photographs here?" I was confident, of course, that he did not.

"Yes," he replied. "We are from *The Tennessean*."

"We?"

"I'm with a reporter who wants to meet with you for about 15 minutes after the service. Pastor Montgomery invited us."

Well, that was a short-lived evangelism career, I thought, angrily contemplating the situation. The newspaper, of all things—that modern day "antichrist" and rival of the truth, the Church, and evangelists in general! They would have a field day at a signs and wonders meeting! Soon, people would be lying all over the floor, defenseless against the camera's all-seeing eye. Something had to be done, and quickly. *Help! God! Help! We have an emergency down here. Red Alert...we have incoming...Code Blue...someone is having a heart attack—me! Come on God, what do You want me to do?*

Nothing, said the voice of the Lord. *It's okay. There is nothing to worry about.*

I clung to those words, *It's okay, it's okay, it's okay*. That message had to be from God. Who else would think that a secular journalist in a spiritual service was "okay"? In my own congregation, I did not even allow photographers to snap pictures during a wedding service, much less a prayer service. I took a deep breath and let it out. "It's okay."

The photographer continued to shoot. At first, the occasional *click-whir* was not too distracting. However, when it was prayer time and the action picked up, so did the number of shots. *Click-whir, click-whir, click-whir. Click-whir, click-whir, click-whir*. It sounded like bullets ricocheting off a steel drum.

After the service, I met with the reporter. The interview lasted 45 minutes instead of 15. I guessed that *The Tennessean* would run a short column in the Saturday religion section. At least by then, we would be on our way back to Florida.

I was in for another surprise. The next morning, the story was carried on the front page with full-color photographs and a headline that read: "A Revival? Where?" Even more surprising, the article was positive. Someone from the local Episcopal bishop's office said it was the first front-page positive press the Episcopal Church had received in recent memory.

The newspaper article caught the attention of the whole city of Nashville. Attendance increased, and we extended the revival for a third week. The final night of the meeting, 600 people squeezed into the 400-seat church. The response to the altar call was so large—250 people—that they were taken next door to the gymnasium for prayer. As it turned out, God was right: It *was* okay. In fact, it was *more* than okay; it was very, very good. We learned that the secular media is not the enemy. In this revival, as in previous ones, the press helped spread the good news.

Lasting Fruit

Two years after the Nashville revival, I made a return visit. Jessica, a friend we made during the first meeting, invited us and paid for our airline tickets and a rental car. Jessica was still aglow with the revival anointing and still using the gift she received—her prayer language.

Vivian, a mutual friend of ours and Jessica's, drove four hours from Tuscaloosa, Alabama, for our one-night meeting at St. Bartholomew's. She brought her friend Cynthia with her. Why would anyone go to so much trouble for one meeting? Vivian wanted her friend to have the same joy she had received. Cynthia had been bound to a wheelchair ever since a skiing accident years earlier.

Father Ian Montgomery was still the pastor at St. Bartholomew's. Revival had brought long-standing parish issues to the surface, and things had been hard. Nevertheless, Ian was quite adamant about the fact that the meetings were a spiritual turning point for the city. The Friday night meeting was held at St. Bartholomew's even though the parish's feelings about revival were still divided. Nevertheless, the testimony we heard was encouraging.

"My husband never did get the joy," one woman said disappointedly, "but one night on the floor, the Lord called him into the ministry. He told our bishop about a year ago, and this fall we are off to seminary...and, oh...do you remember the man you prayed for with multiple sclerosis? I saw him recently, and he's really doing well."

The worship leader that evening was literally "walking and leaping and praising God." Previously, she had come to the meetings in a wheelchair because of severe injuries sustained in an automobile accident. The doctors had said she was terminal. For the three weeks of the revival meetings, she had soaked in the anointing. Afterward, she had gradually moved from the wheelchair to crutches, then to taking small steps, and eventually to managing a slow jog. Two years later, she stood at the keyboard radiating with an inner light and reflecting the glory of God.

What about "Mother Goose"? At the moment of her prophecy three years before, God had healed her of T. M. J., a disease of the jaw. When she sang, "La la la la la la la," her lips were opening in song for the first time in years. Since then, she has returned to work as a vocalist with the Nashville Symphony.

If "lasting fruit" in changed lives is an identifying mark of true revival, then the Lakeland Revival was the real thing. The evidence is overwhelming: The changes in my life and the lives of my family, the changes in Christ the King parish, and the changed lives and churches everywhere the Lord has led me are undeniable. One thing it has taught us is that God truly is sovereign. He is Lord of the Church, and He is remolding, remaking, and reforming it according to His design. He sends revival to get our attention off ourselves and what *we* are doing and onto Him and what *He* is doing. At the same time, He is inviting us to *join* Him in what He is doing. The choice is ours. There is a warning, however: Flowing with the river of revival will not always be easy. The fire of God will melt away the wax of false religion, our theological assumptions, our smug complacency, and our spiritual pretentiousness. Take it from one who has been there: Revival is not always easy; it is not always comfortable; sometimes it is scary; but it is *always* worth the trip. The blessings far outweigh the pain.

Chapter
Twelve

The Lessons of Revival

For me, revival has been a great Holy Spirit classroom. It has been like sitting at the feet of Jesus as He opened my heart and mind to the truth and ways of God as never before. In the spring of 1993, I knew very little—almost nothing—about revival. I was not prepared for it the night it came to me at Carpenter's Home Church. In fact, I was totally "aclewistic" about it. The fall of revival fire at Christ the King Episcopal Church on Palm Sunday caught me completely by surprise. Scrambling at first, I learned quickly, and one of the things I learned is that our God is a God of surprises. His ways are not our ways, and His thoughts are not our thoughts.[1] He chooses the foolish things of the world to shame the wise, and the weak things of the world to shame the strong.[2]

Six years of flowing with the Spirit in this new move of God have taught me several important principles or characteristics—truths, if

1. See Is. 55:8-9.
2. See 1 Cor. 1:27.

you will—of revival. While every person's individual and specific experiences in revival will be different, I believe that these principles are common to any genuine revival, past or present. What I share here is not at all a comprehensive treatment, but reflects what I have learned from my own experiences in revival.

The Presence of God Takes Priority

When true revival comes, the glory and presence of God take precedence and priority over everything else, even our regular religious routines and practices. At times this may even include such "indispensables" as preaching and teaching. The reading of the Gospel lesson is a vital part of Episcopal liturgy, yet when the fire fell on Palm Sunday, 1993, acknowledging and yielding to the *immediate* manifest presence of God was more important. Although virtually nothing in traditional Episcopalian worship is more important than Holy Communion, I have been in revival meetings in Episcopal churches where the sovereign presence of God has preempted the usual, and we never got around to communion. When *God* is in the house, *everything* else is *secondary*.

This focus on the presence of God changes our priorities. So many things that appear so important to us pale in the light of the glory of God. In my experience, one of the priorities that changed was in the sense of time-consciousness in worship. When revival came, our emphasis shifted from "finishing in an hour" to focusing on praise and worship and soaking in the presence of God. The important thing was being in God's presence, *not* on how long we spent at church. Our personal schedules and routines took a back seat to what God wanted to do. It seemed unimportant to be or do anything other than sit in His presence.

Expect the Unexpected

Revival shatters our paradigms and exceeds anything we can imagine. It almost never arrives in the manner we're looking for or proceeds in the way we expect. Because He is the God of surprises, we must learn to expect God to do the unexpected. Get ready for Him to upset the apple cart. The phenomenon of laughter is a good case in point. On Palm Sunday, 1993, divinely inspired laughter overcame me and others in the congregation during one of the most solemn moments in the liturgy. Unexpected? Absolutely. God does the unexpected because He is God and because He wants to get our attention. Sometimes we take ourselves much too seriously, and God has to shake us out of our religious pretentiousness.

God sends revival to rock our theological boat and bring correction and focus to our doctrine and practice. When God invades our familiar routine and does something unexpected, our faith increases and our knowledge and understanding of who God is and what He is like are expanded. The doctrines we believe and the rites we practice are infused with new meaning and life.

Another aspect of the unexpected is when God brings phenomena, manifestations, or events that cannot be fully understood or adequately explained by human reason. For example, why did God supernaturally "levitate" the young college student at one of the meetings at St. Michael's in Gainesville? What was the purpose? Perhaps it was simply to demonstrate His power. Certainly, it was a sign and wonder that prompted a larger than usual response to the altar call. Sometimes the unexpected provides needed encouragement to God's people, reassuring them of His presence, power, and love.

Revival Awakens the Church

God's primary purpose in revival is to awaken the Church. Revival is not "magic fairy dust" to make all our dreams come true. While it brings new life to the people of God, it does not necessarily renew institutions, congregations, or denominations. The Church is not an institution; it is the Body of Christ. It is not an organization, but a living organism made up of those individuals who have surrendered their lives to Christ in faith and repentance.

It is *this* Church, the *true* Church—not the cold, lifeless "church" of empty tradition and ritual—that God awakens in revival.

One effect of this awakening is that our limited human vision is replaced by God's vision. We begin to see things as God sees them; we look at ourselves and others the way God looks at us. This renewed vision causes us to examine our lives and leads us to repentance. It exposes the attitudes of our hearts—for good or bad—and lays bare sin in the church: unfaithfulness in giving, division, dissension, anger, bitterness, unforgiveness. In revival, the Spirit reveals these things in order to bring about cleansing, healing, forgiveness, and reconciliation.

As awakened believers, we become aware of a genuine desire to change—a desire to become more like Christ. Revival teaches us how to walk by faith, not by sight; and when we walk by faith, we discover that when we trust and obey God, He provides for every need, even when we can't see the way.

Part of the awakening that comes with revival is a renewal of marriage and family relationships and a restoration of unity within the Body of Christ. When we are right with God, our human relationships will be in harmony also.

Revival Focuses on Relationship

Revival takes our attention off the "things" of religion and focuses it on our *relationship* with Jesus Christ. Priority is given to the lordship of Christ over His Church, and the control of man is diminished. Like fire in a wax museum, He burns away our dependence on tradition, our complacency, and our bondage to the ordinary. He melts away our pretensions, exposes sin in our lives, and demands personal holiness. At the same time, revival fills us with the absolute assurance of the love of Jesus. Revival is *always* redemptive in purpose, *never* punitive.

Revival makes us more open to hearing and obeying God. It renews our relationship with the Holy Spirit and teaches us to rely on Him every moment. The result of this renewed relationship is a greater abundance of spiritual fruit in our lives.

God's fire comes to hungry hearts, not historic hearths. When fire comes to a wax museum, the traditions of men are melted away, and the purpose of God is revealed. This sudden revelation may appear as terrible judgment, but it was sent to consume the dross and blow away the chaff from God's holy people. Archaeologists have never discovered the cross of Christ. Calvary's site is disputed, and so is the location of Jesus' tomb. The upper room has long since disappeared, but the fire of Pentecost Day continues to blaze and melt the hearts of disciples in every generation—no matter what their surroundings.

Revival Equips the Church for the Purpose of God

One of the things that revival does is bring a fresh anointing to God's people. This anointing contains the power of God to accomplish the purpose of God. The purpose of this anointing is more than just to make us feel good or to brighten up the Church; God has equipped us to do His work on earth. This is the work of Jesus that He commissioned the Church to continue. Just as Jesus was anointed to "preach good news to the poor...to proclaim freedom for the prisoners and recovery of sight for the blind, to release the oppressed, to proclaim the year of the Lord's favor,"[3] so are we.

Revival empowers and prepares us to minister to people in great need. I discovered this when our church began ministering to the boys at Anchor House. The spiritual, emotional, and psychological needs of so many of those young men were beyond what any church or individual could possibly do apart from the power of God. The fresh anointing from the Lord brought with it the supernatural power to minister effectively to them and others like them. When we learned to open ourselves and flow in the

---

3.   Lk. 4:18-19.

Spirit, He brought healing and wholeness to countless numbers of broken and hurting people.

Revival Draws the Spiritually Hungry

One reason God awakens the Church during revival is to help it prepare for the new influx of people that will result from the move of God. Spiritually hungry people, whether lost, backslidden Christians, or growing Christians who want more of the Lord, gravitate toward the evident activity of God. They are drawn to wherever God is moving and working. Lost people are drawn when they sense that the missing element in their lives—God—is alive and active in a church or in an area that is undergoing revival. This is one of the primary purposes of signs and wonders. Many lost people really want to know that God is real and can make a difference in their lives. They don't see any evidence in the secular world, and sadly, too often, see no evidence in the church either. Revival changes this. The God of surprises is also the God of the impossible, and when people witness the impossible—that which only God can do—they are drawn to it, and in many cases, faith is born.

Revival also restores to the fold many backslidden Christians, those "lost sheep" who have strayed away from the Church and from the Lord for any number of reasons. Their parched souls are stirred by the scent of "fresh water" and "new wine," and the Spirit draws them back into a renewed relationship with Christ.

Many Christians who are already on fire for the Lord naturally seek out the places where the fire is burning so that they can add their flame to it, and not only continue to be renewed, but make themselves available for God to use them as He desires to do. Revival inspires and enables believers to assume their proper roles and ministries in the church.

Churches in revival must be alert or they will be caught unprepared, as ours was, by the heightened spiritual hunger and

166

increased numbers of people that revival will bring inside their doors.

Revival Will Meet With Opposition

There is no revival in history that occurred within an environment of complete peace and tranquillity. The inescapable fact is that revival stirs up opposition. Revival revitalizes the Church and converts sinners, but it also inspires controversy. This is because revival amplifies the spiritual clash between two worlds: the Kingdom of Heaven and the kingdom of this world. When God is moving, it seems that the devil gets nervous. It is as if satan and his minions go on high alert to do all they can to thwart, distract, discredit, or derail whatever God is doing. Revival, however, heightens our awareness of how powerful God is and how impotent satan is by comparison.

Strangely enough, opposition to revival comes most often from *within* the Church, not from without. This is true particularly among clergy and other religious leaders. Those who have the most to lose with change are the ones most prone to oppose it. It is interesting to note that studies of revival show that some of the most vigorous and vocal opponents of any *current* move of God are those who were the leaders, the "movers and shakers" of the *previous* move of God. For this reason, we must always be careful not to insist that just because God did something a certain way *last* time, that He will necessarily do it the same way *this* time! This calls for a spirit and attitude of openness to the work of the Spirit in our lives and in our churches.

In any great move of God, some in the Church will follow; many—perhaps most—will not. The question we each must answer for ourselves is whether we are ready to follow God no matter where He leads and regardless of how many others come along. Opposition is puzzling and painful, but it is part of the price we have to pay for revival. Believe me, *it is worth it!*

Effects of the Lakeland Revival

Lakeland was the launching pad for what many believe to be the most explosive revival since the coming of Christ. That cannot be determined at this point because six years later, the revival is still focused on the Church. It has yet to make a major impact on society, an effect that can be measured only after its fruit has had enough time to grow.

The Lakeland Revival did not really begin in Lakeland, but in the heart of a boy who was born in South Africa in 1961. Young Rodney Howard-Browne had a dream: "When I grow up, I am going to America and change the world for Jesus Christ." It was an unwitting prophecy. Born again at age five, Spirit-filled at eight, and sensing the strong leading of God, as a young man Rodney left South Africa to bring revival to America. He arrived here in 1987, but it was not until 1989 in upstate New York that the signs and wonders of joyous laughter broke out in his meeting. In 1993, at the invitation of pastor Karl Strader, he came to Carpenter's Home Church in Lakeland, Florida, for what turned out to be eight weeks of revival.

While giving testimony at one of those meetings, I spoke a word from the Lord that did not seem terribly important at the time: "This revival will spread like a forest fire. It will die out in the center, but sweep to the ends of the earth." It was, however, exactly what happened.

Pilgrims who come to Lakeland today looking for relics of the 1993 revival are disappointed. The big Carpenter's Home Church auditorium is still there, but the Lord deposited the evidence of revival in human hearts, not in denominations and church buildings. We see the most impressive results in what came *out* of Lakeland, not in what remained. Richard Roberts, president of Oral Roberts University, was touched when he visited Carpenter's. He took the joy back to Tulsa, Oklahoma, where he began to laugh at the school's 40 million dollar debt until it began to shrink. Jack

The Lessons of Revival

Collins, the engineer at Carpenter's, left to start his own ministry, as did many other members. Steve Strader, Karl's son, became copastor of the church, but spends one week a month on the road holding revival meetings.

Christ the King Episcopal Church asked me to resign. The vestry wanted a full-time pastor instead of a pastor/evangelist. Mark Rivera, a deacon and the head of Anchor House, stayed during the nine-month search for a new pastor to help the parish. Eventually, the parish called Rick Gomer, a priest touched in a Rodney Howard-Browne meeting in Washington, D.C., as the new rector.

The revival spread from Lakeland like a forest fire just as predicted. Rodney Howard-Browne, whose primary task was to bring revival to America, launched a worldwide revival ministry based nearby in Tampa, Florida. During his St. Louis crusade, he laid hands on a hungry young Vineyard pastor named Randy Clark. In January of 1994, Randy took the fire to another Vineyard church in Toronto, Canada, led by John Arnott. Soon, what the British newspapers called the "Toronto Blessing" had spread to hundreds of other churches around the world.

A spark from Toronto landed in London at an Anglican church called Holy Trinity, Brompton, and soon it became another base for the move of God. HTB's pastor, Sandy Millar, was host to an Anglican bishop who happened to lay hands on a visiting American named Steve Hill. Steve took the fresh anointing to Pensacola, Florida, where revival fire fell on Father's Day, 1995 at the Brownsville Assembly of God, beginning what has become known as the Brownsville Revival. As remarkable as these famous revivals are, there are thousands and thousands of smaller churches whose ministries have been transformed by the fire that spread from Lakeland.

At the end of 1994, and with my bishop's blessing, I formed Bud Williams Ministries to continue the ministry of revival and evangelism to which God called me during the Lakeland meetings. In the five years that have followed, we have ministered in 12 countries: South Africa, Australia, England, Germany, Denmark, Belgium, Colombia, Canada, Sweden, Norway, Tanzania, and the United States. Responses to the altar calls have exceeded 40,000. We have been welcomed in 18 denominations in more than 100 cities: African Methodist Episcopal, Anglican, Apostolic, Assembly of God, Baptist, Church of Christ, Church of God, Church of God in Christ, Danish Pinsekirken, Disciples of Christ, Dutch Reformed, Episcopal, Independent Charismatic, Methodist, Pentecostal Holiness, Presbyterian, Roman Catholic, and Word of Faith.

St. Michael's Episcopal Church in Gainesville and "St. Kilda's" are still in revival. The pastor at Tableview was brought up on heresy charges by his denomination for allowing this move of God in his church. The charges failed. A traveler from Cape Town who often passes by the Dutch Reformed Church in Tableview said there are so many cars there on Sunday that it causes a traffic jam.

New churches were formed when the new wine was not welcomed by those who preferred the old wine. The Toronto church was booted out of the Vineyard, but continued with revival. Rodney Howard-Browne started a congregation called The River at Tampa Bay with a new style of ministry that includes unlimited worship—four- to five-hour services on Sunday morning, uncompromised preaching, regular altar calls, prayer ministry for everyone every Sunday, and a commitment not to pressure or manipulate the congregation in any way.

Turn the Page...

During the Welsh Revival in 1905, William T. Stead, the editor of the prominent British newspaper, *The Pall Mall Gazette*, and generally regarded as one of the most influential and powerful men of his times, attended some of the meetings. Upon his return, he was interviewed by the *London Methodist Times*. Of the revival,

Mr. Stead concluded:

> "Nothing lasts forever in this mutable world...But if the analogy of all previous revivals holds good, this religious awakening will be influencing for the good the lives of numberless men and women who will be living and toiling and carrying on with this God's world of ours long after you and I have been gathered to our fathers."[4]

The last chapter of revival is never written just as the last chapter of the Book of the Acts of the Apostles was never written. God the Holy Spirit always takes a hands-on approach to His Church and His world. Revival is the hand of God correcting, renewing, improving, and motivating His people to complete the mission of Jesus—to carry the good news to the ends of the earth.

---

4. Rick Joyner, *The World Aflame* (Charlotte, NC: Morning Star Publications), 67.

Other Product From The Rev. Hugh E. "Bud" Williams

"The story of revival in an Episcopal Church," testimony interview, cassette $10
"Revival in Russellville," Meetings at Russellville, Arkansas, video $20
"Danish Delight," Revival Meeting at Pinsekirken, Aarhus, Denmark, video $20
"God's Favorite Sign: Yield," teaching excerpts, video $20
"Chronicles of the Revival," free newsletter to mailing list.

To order or to ask for more information, please write or call:

Bud Williams Ministries
P.O. Box 91777
Lakeland, FL 33804
(941) 853-5516
1-800-853-5516
E-mail: Joelsplace@aol.com
Website: http://members.aol.com/joelsplace

These books are for people on the chase after God.

THE GOD CHASERS (Best-selling Destiny Image book)
by Tommy Tenney.
There are those so hungry, so desperate for His Presence, that they become consumed with finding Him. Their longing for Him moves them to do what they would otherwise never do: Chase God. But what does it really mean to chase God? Can He be "caught"? Is there an end to the thirsting of man's soul for Him? Meet Tommy Tenney—God chaser. Join him in his search for God. Follow him as he ignores the maze of religious tradition and finds himself, not chasing God, but to his utter amazement, caught by the One he had chased.
ISBN 0-7684-2016-4

GOD CHASERS DAILY MEDITATION & PERSONAL JOURNAL
by Tommy Tenney.
ISBN 0-7684-2040-7

THE RELEASE OF THE HUMAN SPIRIT
by Frank Houston.
Your relationship and walk with the Lord will only go as deep as your spirit is free. Many things "contain" people and keep them in a box—old traditions, wrong thinking, religious mind-sets, emotional hurts, bitterness—the list is endless. A New Zealander by birth and a naturalized Australian citizen, Frank Houston has been jumping out of those "boxes" all his life. For more than 50 years he has been busy living in revival and fulfilling his God-given destiny, regardless of what other people—or even himself—thinks! In this book you'll discover what it takes to "break out" and find release in the fullness of your Lord. The joy and fulfillment that you will experience will catapult you into a greater and fuller level of living!
ISBN 0-7684-2019-9

THE ASCENDED LIFE
by Bernita J. Conway.
A believer does not need to wait until Heaven to experience an intimate relationship with the Lord. When you are born again, your life becomes His, and He pours His life into yours. Here Bernita Conway explains from personal study and experience the truth of "abiding in the Vine," the Lord Jesus Christ. When you grasp this understanding and begin to walk in it, it will change your whole life and relationship with your heavenly Father!
ISBN 1-56043-337-X

Available at your local Christian bookstore.

Internet: http://www.reapernet.com

Y ou will enjoy these books from Destiny Image too!